10 Minute Guide to
Quicken® 5

Linda Flanders

SAMS

A Division of Macmillan Computer Publishing

11711 North College, Carmel, Indiana 46032 USA

S0-DTD-185

*To my life partner who gives me tremendous guidance
and support along the way.*

© 1991 by SAMS

FIRST EDITION
FIRST PRINTING—1991

International Standard Book Number: 0-672-30253-5
Library of Congress Catalog Card Number: 91-66260

Publisher: *Richard Swadley*
Publishing Manager: *Marie Butler-Knight*
Managing Editor: *Marjorie Hopper*
Acquisitions Editor: *Mary Terese Cagnina*
Development Editor: *Lisa Bucki*
Manuscript Editor: *Judy J. Brunetti*
Cover Design: *Dan Armstrong*
Production Assistance: *Brad Chinn, Denny Hager, Audra Hershman, Phil Kitchel, Sarah Leatherman, Laurie Lee, Joe Ramon*
Indexer: *Johnna VanHoose*

Special thanks to C. Herbert Feltner for verifying the technical accuracy of this book.

Screen reproductions in this book were created by means of the program Collage Plus from Inner Media, Inc., Hollis, NH.

Printed in the United States of America

Trademarks

Contents

Introduction

Perhaps your spouse or small business partner has just purchased Quicken for your computer and asks that you start using the program to automate your finances. Until now, all you've heard about Quicken was that it was a program that allows users to manage their home and business finances. A few things are certain:

- You need to learn the program quickly.

- You need to identify and learn only the tasks necessary to accomplish your particular goals.

- You need a clear-cut, plain-English guide to learn about the basic features of the program.

The *10 Minute Guide to Quicken 5* is designed to teach you the operations you need in short, easy-to-understand lessons that can be completed in 10 minutes or less.

What Is the 10 Minute Guide?

The 10 Minute Guide series is a new approach to learning computer programs. Instead of trying to teach you everything about a particular software product (and ending up with an 800-page book in the process), the 10 Minute Guide teaches you only about the most often-used features.

Each 10 Minute Guide contains between 20 and 30 short lessons. The 10 Minute Guide teaches you about programs without relying on technical jargon—you'll find only plain English used to explain the procedures in this book. With straightforward, easy-to-follow steps, and special artwork (icons) to call your attention to important tips and definitions, the 10 Minute Guide makes learning a new software program quick and easy.

The following icons help you find your way around the *10 Minute Guide to Quicken 5*:

Timesaver Tips offer shortcuts and hints for using the program more effectively.

Plain English icons identify definitions of new terms.

Panic Button icons appear at places where new users often run into trouble.

Additionally, a table of shortcut keys is included at the end of the book, providing you with a guide to the key combinations that access Quicken options and features quickly and easily.

Specific conventions are used to help you find your way around Quicken as easily as possible:

Numbered steps	Step-by-step instructions are highlighted so that you can easily find the procedures you need to perform basic Quicken operations.

`What you type`	The keys you press and the information you type are printed in bold type and color.
`What you see on-screen`	The text you see on-screen will appear in computer type.
Menu names	The names of Quicken menus, options, and activities are displayed with the first letter capitalized.
Menu selections	The letters you press to pull down menus and activate menu options are printed in bold type.

The *10 Minute Guide to Quicken 5* is organized in 22 lessons, ranging from basic startup to more advanced importing and exporting features. Remember, however, that nothing in this book is difficult. Most users want to start at the beginning of the book with the lesson on starting Quicken and progress (as time allows) through the lessons sequentially.

Who Should Use the *10 Minute Guide to Quicken 5*?

The *10 Minute Guide to Quicken 5* is for anyone who:

- Needs to learn Quicken quickly.

- Doesn't have a lot of time to spend learning a new program.

- Wants to find out quickly whether Quicken will meet his or her computer needs.

- Wants a clear, concise guide to the most important features of the Quicken program.

You say your time is important to you and that you need to make the most of it. The *10 Minute Guide to Quicken 5* will help you learn this extremely popular and powerful program in a fraction of the time you might ordinarily spend struggling with new software.

What is Quicken 5?

Quicken is a home and business finance program that helps keep track of your income and expenses. With Quicken, you can:

- Write and print checks
- Keep track of investments
- Create monthly budgets
- Amortize loans
- Generate detailed reports

Additionally, Quicken automatically reminds you of checks to print with the Billminder feature and enables you to pay bills electronically, although these features are not covered in this 10 Minute Guide.

For Further Reference...

Consult *The First Book of Quicken 5* by SAMS

Lesson 1

Getting Started
with Quicken

In this lesson you'll learn how to start and end a typical
Quicken session. You will also learn how to use the
Main menu and various pull-down menus.

Starting Quicken

If you are using Quicken 5 from a hard disk system and
installed it according to the instructions on the inside front
cover of this book, follow these steps:

1. Start your system.

2. At the c:> prompt, type q and press Enter.

The Main menu appears as shown in Figure 1-1. (Depending on how you installed Quicken, numbers may appear
beside the Main menu choices. The version with the numbers leads to *Function-Key menus*, explained in the next
section, "Using Quicken's Menu Types.")

Highlighted menu
choice

Press the highlighted letter to choose a command

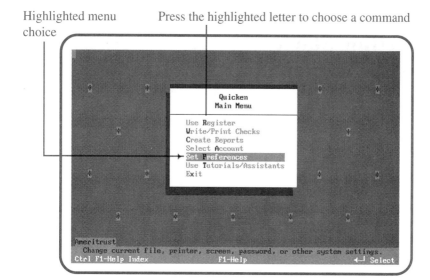

Figure 1-1. The Main menu.

If you are using Quicken 5 from a floppy disk:

1. Start your system.

2. Place the Quicken Program disk in drive A (or drive B if you have two drives). Place your data disk in the other drive.

3. Move to the A:> prompt, if necessary, by typing A: and pressing Enter. Then type Q and press Enter. The Main menu appears as shown in Figure 1-1.

Data Disk. A formatted disk that you use to store Quicken data files.

(Note: The first time that you start the program, Quicken displays the First Time Setup window to select standard categories and the location for your data files. See Lesson 2 for more on setting up Quicken.)

2

Using Quicken's Menu Types

Quicken activities or options are accessed through the Main menu. Quicken 5 includes two menu styles: *Function-Key menus* and *Alt-Key menus*. If you are updating a previous version of Quicken to Quicken 5, the default menu style is the Function-Key menu. If you are installing Quicken for the first time, the default menu style is the Alt-Key menu. This lesson explains both menu styles. For the rest of this book, lessons will be explained using the Alt-Key menu style.

Using Function-Key Menus

You can select program options from a Function-Key menu (such as the one shown in Figure 1-2b) as follows using one of the following methods:

- Press the number or letter that corresponds to the activity or option that you want to select. For example, to select Create Reports, press 3.

- Move the cursor using the Up and Down Arrow keys to the option you want to select. Press Enter. For example, to select the Write/Print Checks option, move the cursor to the `Write/Print Checks` line and press Enter.

- Press a shortcut (Ctrl-key) combination. Shortcut keys are listed on the inside back cover. For example, to select the Use Register option, press Ctrl-R. (Not all Main menu options can be accessed using a shortcut key.)

Press Alt plus the highlighted
letter to pull down a menu

Shortcut keys

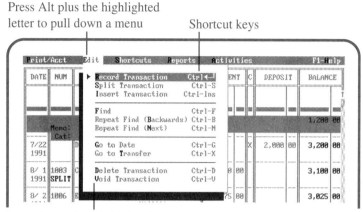

Press the highlighted letter to
select a command

a)   The Alt-Key menu style.

Press the number to
select a command

Press the specified function
key to pull down the menu

Shortcut keys

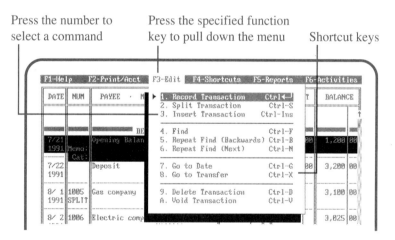

b)   The Function-Key menu style.

Figure 1-2. The pull-down Edit Menu from the
Register screen.

Using Alt-Key Menus

You can select program options from Alt-Key menus (such as the one shown in Figure 1-2a) using one of the following methods:

- Press the highlighted letter in the menu or option name. For example, to select Use **R**egister, press R.

- Move the cursor using the Up and Down Arrow keys to the option that you want to select and press Enter. For example, to select the Select **A**ccount option, move the cursor to the `Select Account` line and press Enter.

Using Pull-Down Menus

After you've selected one of the Main menu options, Quicken displays the opening screen for that activity. Some screens offer pull-down menus to access program options.

Pull-Down Menu. A menu that remains hidden within a menu bar until you use the keyboard to open or *pull down* the complete menu. The complete menu contains additional options, features, and functions. After you access the pull-down menu, you may select any of the options.

To select an option, feature, or function from a Quicken pull-down menu, press the highlighted letter within the option name or press the Alt key in combination with the highlighted letter within the option name. If you are using a mouse, point and click on the option name.

For example, to select the Void Transaction option from the Register screen, follow these steps:

1. Select the account you want to work with. (Lesson 3 explains how to set up and select accounts. You might even want to create a sample account to try out this pull-down menu selection procedure.)

2. Press Alt-E to pull down the Edit pull-down menu as shown in Figure 1-2.

3. Press V to select the Void Transaction option from the Edit pull-down menu.

Using Shortcut Keys. Many options in pull-down menus can be selected using shortcut keys. A shortcut key is a combination of the Ctrl key and a letter key pressed simultaneously. There is no need to access the pull-down menu to use shortcut keys. Simply press the shortcut keys from a register screen, the Write Checks screen, a Report screen, or a Budget screen.

Using the Keyboard

Your keyboard can be used to select menu options and commands and to move around Quicken screens.

Throughout the remainder of this book, the term *select*, for keyboard users, will mean one of the following:

- Press the highlighted letter in the menu or option name.

- Move the cursor to the menu or option name and press Enter.

Using a Mouse

Mouse support is now available with Quicken 5. Any Microsoft-compatible mouse can be used to select menu commands and options, pull-down menus, move around the screen, display windows, or select items from lists. To perform most Quicken operations with a mouse, simply point and click.

Point and Click. To point to an item on the screen, move the mouse pointer to highlight the item on the screen. Then press and release (click) the left mouse button.

This book will explain *keyboard* steps for performing operations in Quicken. Therefore, if you are using a mouse, note the following procedures:

Operation	Mouse Procedure
Open a window	Click the label on the screen
Choose an item from a list	Double-click
Scroll up or down a register or a list	Hold down the mouse on a transaction or list item and move the mouse up or down.
	Hold down the mouse button on a vertical scroll bar arrow
Move to the next or previous transaction or list item	Click the arrows on a vertical scroll bar
Page up or page down a screen	Click on either side of the scroll box
Select options	Click on the option to toggle back and forth

Figure 1-3 shows the vertical scroll bar arrow and box on a register screen.

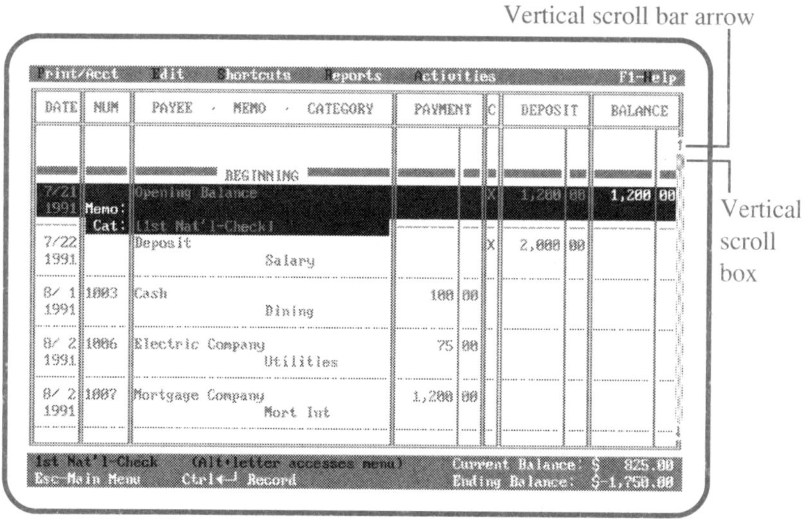

Vertical scroll bar arrow

Figure 1-3. The vertical scroll bar arrow and the vertical scroll box.

For the remainder of this book, the term *select* (for mouse users) will mean to point and click on the item.

Backing Up Your Data Files

Although Quicken automatically saves the data from your work session when you edit, it's wise to keep backup copies of all financial data. To make a backup of your data files before exiting Quicken, follow these steps:

1. Press Esc to return to the Main menu (if necessary).

2. Press Ctrl-E at the Main menu to access the backup option.

3. Place your backup disk in drive A or B.

4. Type the drive letter for your backup disk. Press Enter.

5. Quicken displays the list of Quicken data files. Select the file that you want to back up, and press Enter to begin the backup process.

Backing Up without Exiting. Press Ctrl-B from the Main menu to back up your files without exiting Quicken. Then follow the backup process.

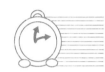

Automatic Backup Reminders. Quicken 5 reminds you to back up your data at intervals that you specify. Quicken gives you the options of being reminded each time you run Quicken weekly, or monthly. Select these options by setting preferences. (See Lesson 2 to learn how to set preferences.)

Exiting Quicken

To exit Quicken and automatically save your data files:

1. Press Escape to return to the Main menu (if necessary).

2. Press X to select Exit from the Main menu. Quicken saves your data files and returns you to the DOS prompt.

Unsaved Data. If you turn your computer off before exiting Quicken through the Main menu, you may lose some of your data. Although Quicken reconstructs some files the next time it is used, complete reconstruction of data files is not possible.

Lesson 2

Setting Up Quicken and Getting Help

In this lesson you will learn how to set preferences (program options) and how to use Quicken's on-screen help system.

Setting Preferences

Quicken allows you to customize the program to better fit your needs by setting preferences for items such as screen settings, printer settings, passwords, electronic payment settings, and more.

To set preferences, follow these steps:

1. Select Set **P**references from the Main menu.

2. Quicken displays the Set Preferences menu.

3. From the Set Preferences menu, select:

   The **P**rinter Settings option to assign printer settings for check printing and report printing. (See Lesson 18.)

The **S**creen Settings option to tell Quicken the type of monitor you are using and to set display options. You can also specify which type of menu you want to use, Alt-key or Function key.

The Password Settings option to assign file and transaction passwords.

The Automatic **R**eminder Settings option to turn Quicken's Billminder feature on or off and to specify the number of days in advance to be reminded of checks to print.

The **T**ransaction Settings option to provide instructions for handling transactions entered in Quicken. For example, if you want Quicken to request confirmation when a transaction is modified, you can choose this option from the Transaction Settings menu. You can also tell Quicken not to beep when recording transactions or performing amortization calculations.

The **C**hecks and Reports Settings option to provide instructions for printing checks and reports. For example, if you want the category name printed on voucher checks, you can choose this option from the Checks and Reports Settings menu.

The Electronic Payment Settings option to set up Quicken to pay bills electronically through CheckFree.

Using Quicken with Windows. You can set up Quicken to work with Microsoft Windows 286, 386, or 3.0 as a nonwindows application. (Refer to your Quicken user manual for more information.)

Using Quicken's Help System

Quicken 5 now offers a fully-indexed, topical Help system. To access a Quicken Help screen, follow these steps:

1. From anywhere in Quicken, press F1 or Alt-H. Quicken displays a window of information about the current screen.

2. If a topic, within the information window, is boldfaced or colored, you can move the cursor to the topic and press Enter to display an additional window of information related to that topic only. For example, in Figure 2-1, you see the Help window displayed from the Write Checks screen. When you move the cursor to the Write a check line and press Enter, the screen shown in Figure 2-2 is displayed with Help information on writing checks.

Move the cursor to a topic and press Enter to display additional help

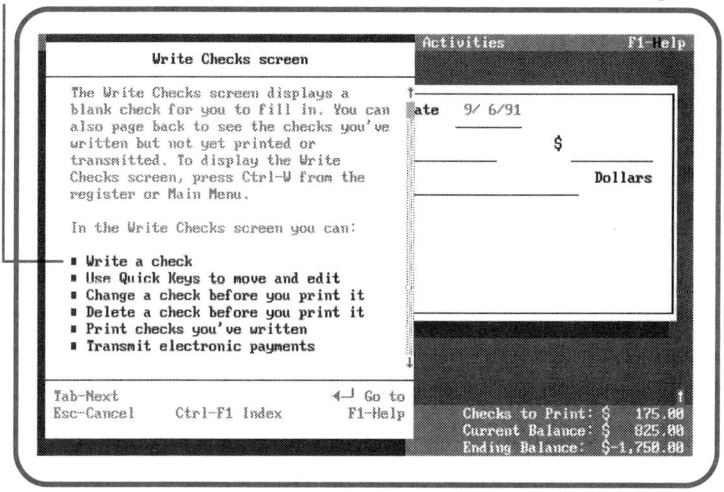

Figure 2-1. The Write Checks Help screen.

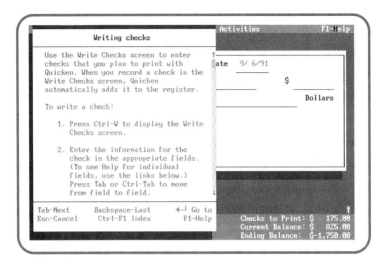

Figure 2-2. The Writing Checks Help screen displayed after selecting `Write a check` from the Write Checks Help screen.

3. To remove the Help window from the screen, press the Esc key.

Using the Help Index

Quicken's Help system is indexed by topic. To locate a topic using the Help index, follow these steps:

1. Press Ctrl-F1 from anywhere in Quicken.

2. Quicken displays the Help Index window shown in Figure 2-3.

Move the cursor to a topic in the index to display the
Help screen for that topic.

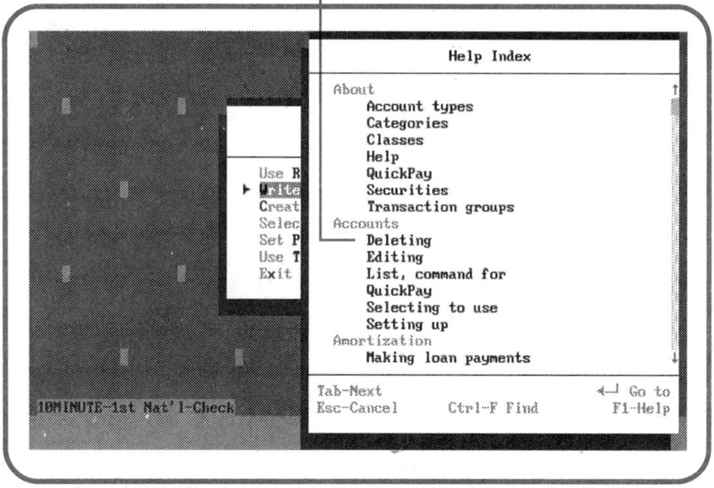

Figure 2-3. Topics listed in the Help Index window.

3. Move around the Help Index using the Up and Down
   Arrow keys, the PgDn and PgUp keys, or the Tab key.

4. Use the following keys to locate topics:

   Tab - moves to the next boldfaced or colored topic.

   Alphabet key - moves to the first topic that begins with
   that letter.

   Ctrl-F - displays the Find window to type a word or
   phrase to search for.

   Backspace - returns to the Help message you just left.

5. When you've located the topic that you need help with,
   press Enter to display the Help screen for that topic.

Accessing the Help Table of Contents

Quicken's basic tasks are listed in the format of a table of contents. To access the table of contents, follow these steps:

1. From anywhere in Quicken, press F1 twice.

2. Quicken displays a table of contents (see Figure 2-4) that you can use to select a task that you need help with.

Move the cursor to a task to display the Help screen for that task.

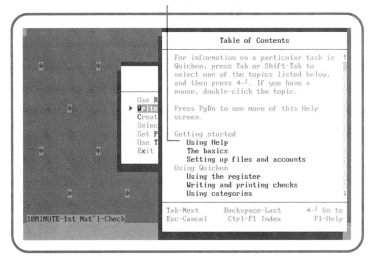

Figure 2-4. The Help Table of Contents listing Quicken's basic tasks.

3. Select the task that you need help with and press Enter to display the Help screen for that topic.

Using Tutorials and Assistants

Quicken 5's Tutorials and Assistants option provides you with an overview of the program and serves as an on-screen demonstration for first-time setup procedures. To use Tutorials and Assistants, follow these steps:

1. Select Use Tutorials/Assistants from the Main menu to display the Tutorials and Assistants menu.

2. Select:

   First Time SetUp if you are a new Quicken user and need help getting started.

   See Quicken Overview if you want a brief presentation on the program features.

   Set Up Quick Tour if you want to experiment with Quicken and enter the sample data from the Quicken User Manual.

   Create New File if you need help setting up a Quicken file.

   Create New Account if you want assistance in setting up an account.

   Create Payroll Support if you want Quicken to set up payroll categories and accounts that you can use in your small business.

3. Follow the on-screen prompts.

Lesson 3

Setting Up Accounts

In this lesson, you'll learn how to set up and select the accounts that you will use in Quicken.

Before you can start using Quicken to record transactions, you must set up the accounts that you will use to track your financial activity.

Accounts and Transactions. An account is an individual record of financial transactions. Transactions increase or decrease the balance in any given account.

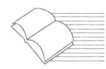

Types of Accounts

The following is a list of the six account types that you can use to track your financial activity. Each account description contains a reference to the lesson that teaches you about working with that account type.

- **Bank.** This is the most commonly used account type. It includes checking, savings, or money market accounts. (See Lesson 4.)

- **Credit Card**. These accounts keep track of your credit card transactions. (See Lesson 15.)

- **Cash**. Cash accounts keep track of your cash expenditures. (See Lesson 16.)

- **Other Asset**. Use this account type to record and track the value of things that you own, such as your home or auto. (See Lesson 17.)

- **Other Liability**. This account type records and tracks the debts that you owe, such as the mortgage on your home or the outstanding loan balance on your auto. (See Lesson 17.)

- **Investment**. Use this type to track investments such as stocks, bonds, and mutual funds. Because this account type represents one of Quicken's more advanced features, it will not be covered in this book. See your Quicken user manual for more information.

Setting Up an Account

To set up any one of the six Quicken account types:

1. Press A to choose Select Account from the Main menu or press Ctrl-A to display the Select Account to Use window.

2. Using the Up Arrow key, move the arrow to the <New Account> line on the Select Account to Use screen (see Figure 3-1) and press Enter.

3. Quicken displays the Set Up New Account screen as shown in Figure 3-2.

Quick Key for easy access to an account

Number of transacations in the register for an account

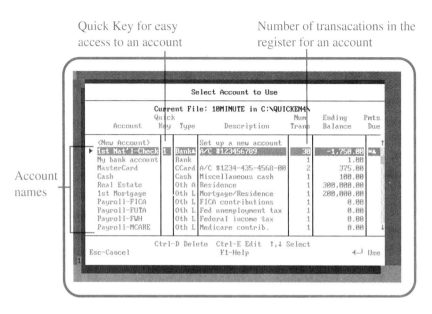

Account names

Figure 3-1. The Select Account to Use screen.

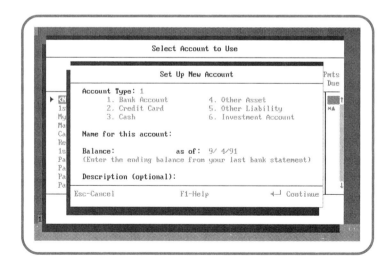

Figure 3-2. The Set Up New Account screen.

4. Type the following to select an account:

   1 for Bank Account
   2 for Credit Card
   3 for Cash
   4 for Other Asset
   5 for Other Liability
   6 for Investment Account

5. Press Enter.

6. Type the name for the account and press Enter. For example, if you are setting up a bank account, the account name you enter might be `First National`. Account names may be up to 15 characters in length and may include spaces, numbers, or other characters except [ ] / : .

7. Enter the balance of your account and press Enter.

Entering a Balance. For bank accounts, enter the balance in your bank account on the day you set up the account. For credit card accounts, enter the balance due from your last statement. Enter the amount of cash on hand for cash accounts. For other asset accounts, enter the current value of the asset. For other liability accounts, enter the current principal portion, plus accrued interest, of the liability.

8. Type the date that relates to the balance entered in Step 7 and press Enter. (Note: You may override the default system date.)

9. Type a description of the account and press Enter. Descriptions are optional and may be up to 20 characters in length. Examples of descriptions you may want to use are the account number of your bank account or credit card, or the street address of real estate.

The account that you have just set up is entered in the Select Account to Use screen.

Selecting an Account to Use

Quicken records transactions in an electronic register for each account. Before you can write checks or enter transactions into a register, you must tell Quicken which account you want to use. To select an account, follow these steps:

1. Press A to choose Select Account from the Main menu or press Ctrl-A to display the Select Account to Use window.

2. Using the Up and Down Arrow keys, move the arrow to the account that you want to use on the Select Account to Use window and press Enter. Quicken accesses the register for the account that you select.

Electronic Register. An electronic register is an on-screen register that lists the date and amount of a transaction, the payee, and the current balance in the account. Electronic registers are very similar to your manual check register.

Selecting an Account. To avoid scrolling through a long list of Quicken accounts, type the first letter of the account name that you want to select. Quicken highlights the first account name that begins with that letter.

Assigning Quick Keys to Accounts

Quicken 5 enables you to assign your own Quick key to the accounts that you use most often. With the use of Quick keys, you can select an account from any screen by pressing the Ctrl key in combination with the Quick key that you assigned to the account. To assign a Quick key to an account, follow these steps:

1. Press A to choose Select Account from the Main menu or press Ctrl-A to display the Select Account to Use window.

2. Using the Up and Down Arrow keys, move the arrow to the account to which you want to assign a Quick key.

3. Press Ctrl-E to access the Edit Account Information window.

4. Assign a number from 1-9 in the Quick Key Assignment field.

5. Press Ctrl-Enter to record the Quick Key assignment.

Editing an Account

After you have set up an account, you can make changes to the account name and/or the account description. To edit an account, follow these steps:

1. Using the Up and Down Arrow keys, move the arrow to the account that you want to edit on the Select Account to Use window.

2. Press Ctrl-E to select the Edit option.

3. Type over the account name and/or the account description.

4. Press Enter to save the changes to the account.

Deleting an Account

You can delete accounts from the Quicken account list. However, once deleted, the account is permanently removed and cannot be restored. To delete an account, follow these steps:

1. Using the Up and Down Arrow keys, move the arrow to the account that you want to delete on the Select Account to Use window.

2. Press Ctrl-D to select the Delete option.

3. Quicken displays a caution that a deleted account will be permanently removed. Type YES if you are sure that you want to delete the account.

4. Press Enter to delete the account.

23

Lesson 4

Working with Bank Accounts

In this lesson you'll learn how to set up a bank account that you can use to write and print checks and/or enter other transactions such as deposits and ATM withdrawals.

Setting Up a Bank Account

A *bank account* is a Quicken account used to write and print checks. Bank accounts include checking, savings, or money market accounts.

To set up a bank account (see Lesson 3 for an explanation on setting up a new account), follow these steps:

1. Press 1 to select Bank Account in the Account Type field found in the Set Up New Account screen and press Enter.

2. Type the name of the account and press Enter. Usually, this will be the name of the bank and/or the type of bank account. For example, you might enter `1st Nat'l-Check` to denote that the account is a checking account with 1ST National Bank.

3. Type the starting balance in your account and press Enter. This is the account balance as of the date that you specify (in the next step) as the start date.

The balance that you show in your checking or savings register may be different than the balance that your bank shows in your account. Bank service charges and/or interest earned are usually debited or credited to your account on the date that your bank generates your statement. To accurately reflect your bank account balance, set up your Quicken bank account after receiving a statement from your bank and enter the balance as shown on your statement. Remember, however, to enter any uncleared transactions (that is, checks not cleared by the bank or deposits not credited to your account) in the Quicken check register. (See Lesson 5 to learn how to enter transactions into the check register.)

4. Type the date that relates to the starting balance that you entered in Step 3 and press Enter. If you are using your last bank statement balance, enter the statement date.

5. Type a description (optional) of the account. If you have more than one checking or savings account with the same bank, it would be useful to enter an account number here. Figure 4-1 shows the Set Up New Account screen with sample data entered.

6. Press Enter to add the bank account to the Quicken account list. Figure 4-2 shows the example account added to the Select Account to Use screen.

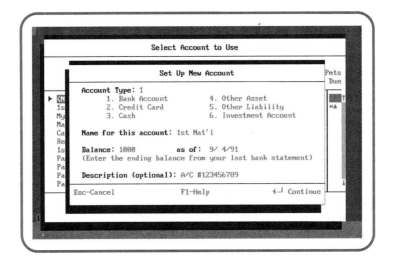

Figure 4-1. The Set Up New Account Screen with sample data entered.

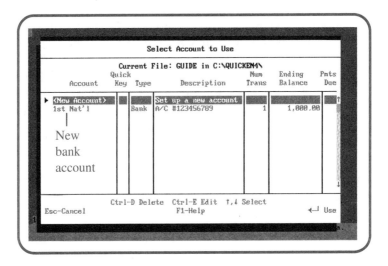

Figure 4-2. The Select Account to Use screen with a bank account added.

Lesson 5
Using the
Check Register

In this lesson you'll learn how to use the Quicken check register to record all of the activity that affects your bank account balance.

Accessing the Check Register

The Quicken check register is similar to a manual check register by the way it records all bank account activity.

Check Register. A check register pertains specifically to a bank account. The check register lists the date of a transaction, the check number, payee, payment amount, deposit amount, memo message (optional), category (optional), status of the transaction (whether it has cleared the bank), and the remaining balance in the account.

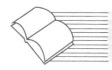

If you write checks using Quicken, your transactions are automatically recorded in the check register. Deposits, ATM withdrawals, adjustments, bank service charges, and interest earned on bank accounts are entered directly into the check register. Quicken adjusts your bank account balance for each transaction entered.

To access the Quicken check register:

1. Press A to choose Select **A**ccount from the Main menu.

2. Select the bank account to use. (Refer to Lesson 3.)

3. Quicken displays the Check Register screen as shown in Figure 5-1.

Enter new transactions
in the highlighted area

Calculated account balance
after a transaction

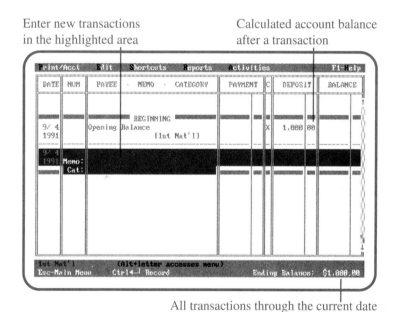

All transactions through the current date

Figure 5-1. The Check Register screen.

Quick Access. If you have already selected the bank account that you want to use and have performed another function (printed reports, written checks, etc.), access the check register by pressing Ctrl-R.

Entering Transactions into the Check Register

To enter new transactions in the blank transaction line at the end of the check register:

1. Access the bank account check register as described earlier in this lesson.

2. Enter the date, check number (if applicable), payee, payment or deposit amount, memo, and category. Press the Tab key or the Enter key to move to each field.

3. Press Ctrl-Enter or F10 to record the transaction.

Entry Shortcuts

You can quickly change a transaction date by pressing the + or – keys, moving the date up or back. Press the + key to enter the next check number. Use the + or – keys to change the check number. For example, if the check number shown is 1066, press the – key to change the check number to 1065. Quicken 5 offers a few more options for quick entry in the Date field as follows:

- Press T to change the date to today's date.
- Press M to change the date to the first day of the current month.
- Press H to change the date to the last day of the current month.

- Press Y to change the date to the first day of the current year.

- Press R to change the date to the last day of the current year.

 Inserting Transactions. With Quicken 5 you can insert transactions anywhere in the register, not just at the end. Position the highlight bar on a transaction with the same date as the transaction that you want to enter and press Ctrl-Ins.

Finding Transactions in the Check Register

To quickly find a transaction without scrolling through the entire check register:

1. From the Check Register screen, press Alt-E to access the Edit pull-down menu and select Find, or just press Ctrl-F.

2. Type the information that matches the transaction that you are searching for in the Transaction to Find window shown in Figure 5-2. You can ask Quicken to find transactions that match payment or deposit amounts, payees, memos, or categories. Press Ctrl-D to clear the Transaction to Find window.

3. Press Ctrl-B to search backwards or Ctrl-N to search forward. Continue pressing Ctrl-B or Ctrl-N until you have found the transaction that you are looking for.

Enter information to help Quicken find a transaction in the register

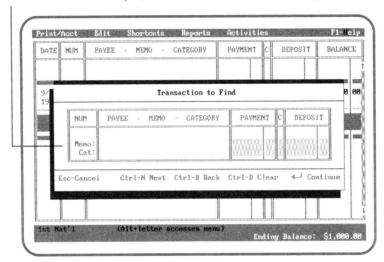

Figure 5-2. The Transaction to Find window.

Unfound Transaction. If you ask Quicken to search for a transaction and a message appears stating that no transaction was found, check to make sure you entered the information correctly in the Transaction to Find window.

Key Word Matches. If you are unsure of the exact words or phrases used in the transaction you are trying to find, enter double periods (..) before or after a key word. For example, if you know that the name of a payee contains the word "Market," type `market..` and Quicken will find transactions that begin with the word market, such as Market Research, Inc. or Market Developers, Inc.

Moving to a Specific Date

To find transactions in the check register that occurred on a specific date, follow these steps:

1. From the Check Register screen, press Alt-E to access the **E**dit pull-down menu and select **G**o to Date, or press Ctrl-G.

2. Type the date in the Go to Date window or press the + or – keys to change the date forward or backwards.

3. Press Enter. Quicken finds the first transaction with the date that you entered in the Go to Date window.

Editing a Transaction in the Check Register

You can make changes to a transaction that you have entered in the check register. You cannot, however, edit or change the amount calculated in the remaining balance column of the check register. To edit a transaction:

1. Access the bank account check register, as explained earlier in this lesson.

2. Use the Up and Down Arrow keys, PgUp and PgDn keys, or the Home and End keys to move the highlight bar to the transaction that you want to edit.

3. Press the Tab or the Enter key to move to the field that you want to edit.

4. Make the necessary change(s) and press Ctrl-Enter or F10 to save the changes.

Deleting a Transaction in the Check Register

To delete a transaction from the check register:

1. Access the bank account check register, as explained earlier in this lesson.

2. Use the Up and Down Arrow keys, PgUp and PgDn keys, or the Home and End keys to move the highlight bar to the transaction that you want to delete.

3. Press Alt-E to access the Edit pull-down menu and select Delete Transaction, or just press Ctrl-D.

4. At the OK to Delete Transaction window, press 1 to select Delete Transaction to remove the transaction from the check register. (Note: If you have not set the transaction setting for confirming deleted or voided transactions to Y (Yes), Quicken will not display the OK to Delete Transaction window; the transaction will be deleted immediately after you select Delete Transaction. See Lesson 2 for more on transaction settings.)

In this lesson you learned how to use the Quicken check register to record, edit, and delete transactions. In the next lesson you'll learn how to use the program calculator to amortize loans.

Using the Calculator and the Loan Calculator

In this lesson you'll learn how to use Quicken's on-screen calculator and the new loan calculator to amortize loans.

Accessing the Calculator

To access the Quicken calculator, follow these steps:

1. From the Write Checks screen or any register screen, press Alt-A to access the **A**ctivities pull-down menu.

2. Press C to select **C**alculator to display the Quicken calculator as shown in Figure 6-1.

   Quick Access. You can access the on-screen calculator at any time in Quicken simply by pressing Ctrl-O.

Click the calculator's keypad with the mouse

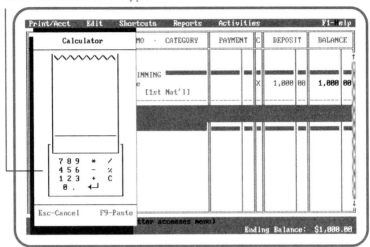

Figure 6-1. The Quicken calculator.

Using the Calculator

The on-screen calculator adds, subtracts, multiplies, and divides numbers. To use the calculator, follow these steps:

1. Access the Quicken calculator, as explained earlier in this lesson.

2. Enter the first number in your calculation. What you enter appears in the cursor line until you press an arithmetic sign or Enter.

3. Press one of the following:

   + to add a number
   – to subtract a number
   / to divide a number
   * to multiply a number

4. Enter the other numbers and arithmetic signs to continue your calculation.

5. Press Enter to complete and total your calculation.

Chain Calculations. To enter the last total calculated (after you have pressed Enter) in a subsequent calculation, press + or * and Quicken enters the last total amount as the first number in your next calculation.

Clearing the Calculator

To clear the last calculation from the calculator, press C to select **C**lear.

Using Percentages

To add or subtract a percentage from a number, follow these steps:

1. Enter the number that you want to add a percentage to or subtract a percentage from.

2. Press + to add or – to subtract.

3. Enter the percentage that you want to add or subtract.

4. Type % to convert the last number entered to a percentage.

5. Press Enter to calculate the total.

Pasting (Copying) Calculations

Using the Paste feature, you can enter the calculated amount from the on-screen calculator into an amount field in the Quicken program. To paste or copy a calculated amount into Quicken, follow these steps:

1. Position the cursor on the Amount field that you want to copy a calculated number to.

2. Press Ctrl-O to access the Quicken calculator.

3. Perform your calculation.

4. Press F9 to select Paste to copy the calculated amount to the amount field.

After you paste an amount to the amount field, Quicken clears the calculator from the screen.

Closing the Calculator

When you finish using the calculator, simply press Esc to clear the screen. The last calculation performed will appear the next time you access the calculator.

Accessing the Loan Calculator

Quicken 5 enables you to amortize loans with its new on-screen loan calculator. With the loan calculator, you can perform "what if" calculations to determine the effect of changes in interest rates, principal amounts, and payment periods. To access the loan calculator, follow these steps:

1. From the Write Checks screen or any register screen, press Alt-A to access the Activities pull-down menu.

2. Press L to select Loan Calculator and display the Quicken loan calculator as shown in Figure 6-2.

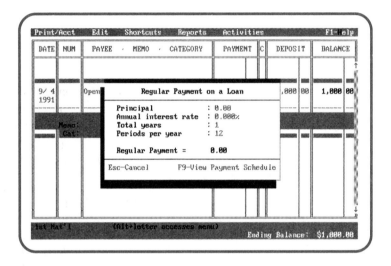

Figure 6-2. The loan calculator.

Using the Loan Calculator

To amortize loans using the loan calculator, follow these steps:

1. Access the loan calculator as just explained.

2. Type the principal amount of the loan, the annual interest rate (up to four decimal places), the total years (period of time that the loan covers), and the number of periods (payments) per year.

3. After you enter the information in the loan calculator, Quicken calculates the payment amount and displays it in the Regular Payment field at the bottom of the calculator.

4. Press Esc to clear the loan calculator from the screen.

Viewing the Payment Schedule

After you calculate the loan payment using the loan calculator, you can view the payment schedule. The payment schedule lists the payment number, interest and principal allocated to each payment, and the remaining principal balance. To view the payment schedule, follow these steps:

1. Calculate the regular payment amount using the loan calculator as just explained.

2. Press F9 to display the Approximate Payment Schedule window. You can move up and down the window to view the entire payment schedule.

Printing the Payment Schedule

To print the Loan Payment schedule, follow these steps:

1. Display the Approximate Payment Schedule window for a loan as just explained.

2. Press Ctrl-P to print the Loan Payment schedule and type the number of the printer that you are using.

Lesson 7

Setting Up and Assigning Categories

In this lesson you'll learn how to set up and assign categories to transactions.

Setting Up Categories

Quicken includes preset, standard home and business categories. You choose which category list (home or business) you want to use when you setup Quicken account files. (See Lesson 22.) You can add, edit, or delete categories from the standard category lists.

Category. Categories are groupings of income and expenses; they are used to classify your transactions for budgeting and income tax reporting purposes. For example, you may categorize your expenses into the following groups: rent, utilities, groceries, medical, entertainment, etc.

Adding a Category

To add a new category, follow these steps:

1. From the Write Checks screen or any register screen, press Alt-S to access the **S**hortcuts pull-down menu and select **C**ategorize/Transfer, or just press Ctrl-C.

2. Quicken displays the Category and Transfer List as shown in Figure 7-1.

Category/Subcategory names

Indicates categories/subcategories that are tax-related

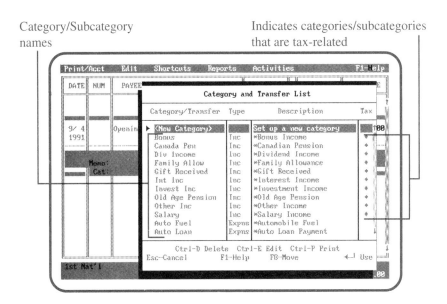

Figure 7-1. The Category and Transfer List.

3. Press Home to move to the `<New Category>` line and press Enter.

4. Quicken displays the Set Up Category screen as seen in Figure 7-2.

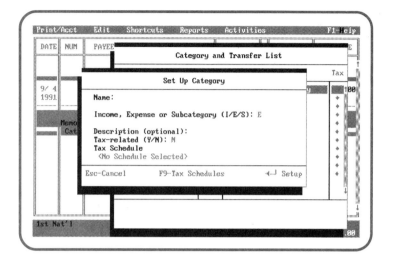

Figure 7-2. Use the Set Up Category screen to add a new category.

5. Type the name of the category and press Enter. Category names can be up to 15 characters (including spaces), but cannot include : / [ ].

6. Press one of the following:

   I for income categories
   E for expenses categories
   S for subcategories

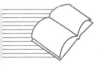

Subcategory. A subcategory further divides a category into a secondary category. For example, you might divide a medical category by setting up subcategories like hospital, doctor, drugs, and so on.

7. Type a category description and press Enter. (Note: Category descriptions appear in report headings.)

Category Names. If you prefer to have the category names appear on your reports instead of the category descriptions, change the checks and reports setting from the Set Preferences menu. (Refer to Lesson 2 to learn more on how to change checks and reports settings.)

8. Type γ if the category is tax-related. All categories designated as tax-related will appear on the Personal Tax Summary Report.

9. If you want to assign a tax schedule to this category, press F9. Quicken displays the Tax Schedule window. Use the Up and Down Arrow keys to position the highlight bar on the tax schedule for this category and press Enter. Quicken next displays the Tax Line window. Scroll through the window to select the description of the tax line for this category and press Enter to enter the Tax Schedule name on the Set Up Category screen. (Note: You cannot edit the Tax Schedule field directly; you must access the Tax Schedules window by pressing F9.)

10. Press F10 to add the new category to the Category and Transfer List.

Adding Categories While Entering Transactions. You can add a new category from the Write Checks screen or any register screen while you are entering transactions. Press Ctrl-C to access the Category and Transfer List. Then follow the steps just explained to add a new category.

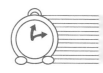

Using Tax Schedules. Quicken 5 lets you assign a tax schedule to each category. Then, at the end of the year you can run a Tax Schedule report to summarize all of your transactions by tax schedule. If you prepare your own income taxes, this feature will give you everything you need to transfer amounts to the related tax form or schedule. For example, Dividend Income is reported on Schedule B of Form 1040. You can assign the Dividend Income category to Schedule B and at the end of the year, all transactions assigned to the Dividend Income category will appear under the Schedule B heading of the Tax Schedule report.

Editing a Category

Quicken enables you to make changes to existing categories. To edit a category, follow these steps:

1. Select **C**ategorize/Transfer from the **S**hortcuts pull-down menu, or press Ctrl-C to access the Category and Transfer List.

2. Use the Up and Down Arrow keys to move the arrow to the category that you want to edit.

3. Press Ctrl-E to access the Edit Category screen.

4. Make the necessary changes to the Edit Category screen.

5. Press Enter to save the changes.

Deleting a Category

You can delete categories from the Category and Transfer List at any time. To delete a category, follow these steps:

1. Select the **Categorize/Transfer** option from the Short-cuts pull-down menu or press Ctrl-C to access the Category and Transfer List.

2. Use the Up and Down Arrow keys to move the arrow to the category that you want to delete.

3. Press Ctrl-D to select the **D**elete option.

4. Quicken displays a warning stating that you are about to permanently delete a category.

5. Press Enter to delete the category.

Changing Categories and Subcategories

Quicken 5 allows you to change a category to a subcategory (demote a category) or change a subcategory to a category (promote a subcategory) or move a subcategory to another category. For example, you may decide to make the category *Auto Fuel* a subcategory of *Auto*. The Move feature allows you to make this change and Quicken will automatically change the category/subcategory name in each transaction.

Changing a Category to a Subcategory

To change a category to a subcategory, follow these steps:

1. Access the Category and Transfer List window as just explained.

2. Use the Up and Down Arrow keys to highlight the category that you want to change to a subcategory.

3. Press F8 to select the Move option. Quicken moves the category to the top of the Category and Transfer List and places a colon (:) in front of the category name to indicate that it can now be moved (changed).

4. Use the Up and Down Arrow keys to move the category name to the category it is to be a subcategory for. Quicken displays the category name next to the target category name. For example, in the preceding example, after completing this step the category will appear like this:

   ```
   Auto : Auto Fuel
   ```

5. Press Enter to change the category to a subcategory and place the subcategory beneath the category name.

Changing a Subcategory to a Category

To change a subcategory to a category, follow these steps:

1. Access the Category and Transfer List window as just explained.

2. Use the Up and Down Arrow keys to highlight the subcategory that you want to change to a category.

3. Press F8 to select the Move option.

4. Press Home to move the subcategory to the top of the list.

5. Press Enter and Quicken changes the subcategory to a category and positions the name alphabetically in the Category and Transfer List.

Merging Categories/Subcategories

You can merge one category/subcategory into another category/subcategory. For example, you may want to merge the *Interest Income* category into the *Investment Income* category if you find that you are not really using the former category.

When you merge two categories/subcategories, Quicken automatically assigns the category/subcategory name you retain (in this case, Investment Income) to each transaction with the merged category/subcategory (Interest Income). To merge a category/subcategory into another category/ subcategory, follow these steps:

1. From the Category and Transfer List, highlight the category/subcategory that you want to merge into another category/subcategory.

2. Follow the steps just explained to change a category to a subcategory.

3. Highlight the new subcategory and press Ctrl-D to delete the new subcategory from the list.

Printing the Category List

You may want a hard copy of the categories that you have set up to use with Quicken. To print the Category List, follow these steps:

1. Select **C**ategorize/Transfer from the **S**hortcuts pull-down menu, or press Ctrl-C to access the Category and Transfer List.

2. Press Ctrl-P to select the Print option.

3. Type the number of the printer that you are using if it is different than the default.

4. Press Enter to print the Category List.

Assigning Categories to Transactions

You can assign categories to transactions to help track your income and expenses. Assigning categories is optional; Quicken does not require an entry in the Category field. To assign a category to a transaction, follow these steps:

1. Press Ctrl-R to access the check register as explained in Lesson 5. (Note: Categories can also be assigned to transactions from the Write Checks screen. See Lesson 12.)

2. Enter the transaction information: date, check number, payee, payment or deposit amount, and memo.

3. Type the category name in the Category field. You can type the category name in either uppercase or lower-case, regardless of how it was set up in the Category and Transfer List. To assign a subcategory, type : after the category name and then type the subcategory name. (Note: Quicken checks the category/subcategory name that you enter to see if it is in the Category and Transfer List. If not, Quicken gives you the option of selecting another category from the list or creating the new category that you just typed.)

4. Press Ctrl-Enter or F10 to record the transaction.

Assigning Categories by Browsing

If you aren't sure which category/subcategory you want to assign to a transaction, you can browse through the Category and Transfer List and select the category directly from the list. To assign a category from the Category and Transfer List, follow these steps:

1. With the highlight bar on the Category field, select Categorize/Transfer from the Shortcuts pull-down menu, or press Ctrl-C to access the Category and Transfer List.

2. Use the Up and Down Arrow keys to look through the list.

3. Position the arrow on the category/subcategory that you decide to assign to this transaction and press Enter.

4. Quicken enters the category name in the Category field.

5. Press Ctrl-Enter or F10 to record the transaction.

Lesson 8

Working with Split Transactions

In this lesson you will learn how to assign more than one category to a transaction by splitting the transaction.

Splitting Transactions

You can assign more than one category to a transaction, called splitting the transaction. For example, if you withdraw cash to pay for an evening out, you may want to assign three categories (Dining, Entertainment, and Sitter) to the transaction. To split a transaction:

1. Press Ctrl-R from the Main menu to access the check register as explained in Lesson 5. (Note: You can also split transactions in the Write Checks screen. Refer to Lesson 12.)

2. Enter all transaction information and the amount of the transaction into the register.

3. With the highlight bar on the transaction, select Split Transaction from the Edit pull-down menu, or press Ctrl-S to open the Split Transaction window as shown in Figure 8-1.

One transaction has been split
between three categories

Amounts in the Split Transaction window
equal the transaction amount in the register

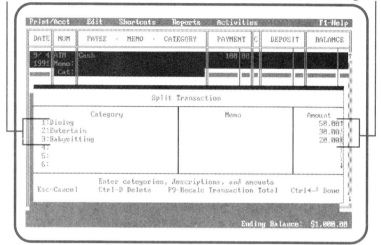

Figure 8-1. You can assign more than one category
to a transaction in the Split Transaction screen.

4. Type the first category name and press Enter.

5. Type a description (optional) and press Enter.

6. Type the amount to be allocated to the first category and
   press Enter. (Note: You can enter positive or negative
   amounts in the Amount field.)

7. Continue entering categories, descriptions, and amounts
   until the total amount of the transaction is allocated to
   categories.

8. Press Ctrl-Enter to finish the split transaction.

9. Quicken returns to the register and enters SPLIT in the
   Check Number field as seen in Figure 8-2. In the Write
   Checks screen, Quicken enters SPLIT below the Category field. (Note: The word SPLIT does not appear on
   the printed check.)

The Register shows when a transaction is split

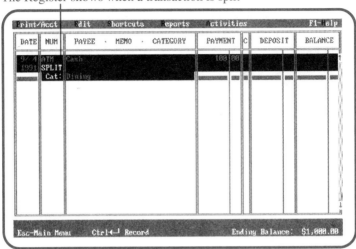

Figure 8-2. A split transaction noted in the register.

 **Calculating Split Transactions.** As you enter each line of a split transaction, Quicken calculates the remaining balance of the transaction and enters the result in the next category line.

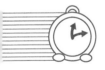 **Copying in the Split Transaction Window.** To copy the main category name from the previous line, type " in the Category field on the next line. Then press Enter.

Splitting Transactions by Percentages

With Quicken 5 you can allocate percentages to split transactions. For example, you may want to allocate an expense between your business and home by percentage; 60% business and 40% home. To split transactions by percentages follow these steps:

1. Follow the steps just explained to open the Split Transaction window for a transaction.

2. Type the category name and memo (optional).

3. Type the percentage in the Amount field. Percentages are entered as 00%. For example, twenty percent is entered as 20%.

4. Press Enter and Quicken multiplies the transaction amount by the percentage and enters the result.

5. Repeat Steps 2 through 4 to split the transaction further.

Editing Split Transactions

You can change the information in a split transaction. To edit a split transaction, follow these steps:

1. Position the highlight bar on the split transaction in the register that you want to edit.

2. Select Split Transaction from the Edit pull-down menu or press Ctrl-S to access the Split Transaction window.

3. Make any necessary changes to the Split Transaction window.

4. Press Ctrl-Enter to record the changes.

Deleting Lines in a Split Transaction

To delete a line in a split transaction, follow these steps:

1. Position the cursor on the line that you want to delete in the Split Transaction window.

2. Press Ctrl-D to delete the line.

(Note: To delete an entire split transaction, you must delete each line from the Split Transaction window and press Ctrl-Enter.)

Recalculating Split Transaction Amounts

If you enter an amount in the register or Write Checks screen for a transaction, you can recalculate the transaction amount using the Split Transaction window. To recalculate the amount, follow these steps:

1. Select Split Transaction from the Edit pull-down menu, or press Ctrl-S to open the Split Transaction window for a transaction.

2. Type the amounts in the Amount column. To subtract, enter a – sign before the amount.

3. After you have entered the amounts that make up the transaction amount, press F9 to select Recalc Transaction Total.

4. Quicken recalculates the transaction total and enters the result in the register as the transaction amount.

In this lesson you learned how to assign more than one category to a transaction. In the next lesson, you'll learn how to use classes and subclasses.

Lesson 9
Using Classes and Subclasses

In this lesson you will learn how to create and use classes and subclasses.

Creating Classes

Using classes in Quicken enables you to specify exactly what information a transaction covers. Unlike categories, Quicken does not provide a preset list of classes.

Class. A class specifies who, where, or what time period a transaction is for. Classes are an extension of categories. For example, if you have a Clothing category set up, you might want to set up a class for each family member to track the amount spent on clothing for each person.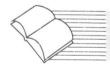

To create a class, follow these steps:

1. From any register screen, choose Select/Set Up Class from the Shortcuts pull-down menu or just press Ctrl-L.

2. Quicken displays the Class List shown in Figure 9-1.

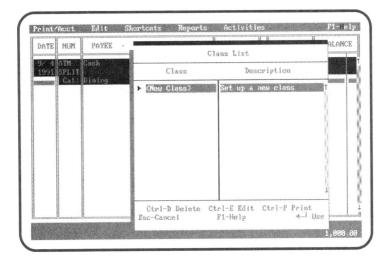

Figure 9-1. The Class List.

3. Press Home to move to the `<New Class>` line, if necessary, and press Enter.

4. Quicken displays the Set Up Class screen as seen in Figure 9-2.

5. Type the name of the class and press Enter. Class names can be up to 15 characters (including spaces), but cannot include : / [ ].

6. Type a class description. (Note: Class descriptions appear in report headings.)

7. Press Enter to add the class to the Class List.

Creating Classes While Entering Transactions.
You can create a new class from the Write Checks screen or any register screen. Press Ctrl-L to access the Class List. Then follow the steps just explained to create a new class.

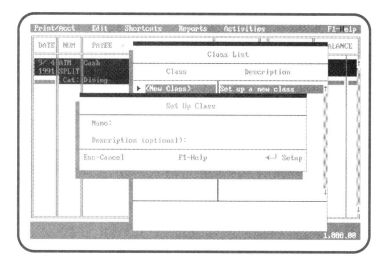

Figure 9-2. Use the Set Up Class screen to create a new class.

Editing a Class

You can make changes to classes that you have already created. To edit a class, follow these steps:

1. Choose Select/Set Up Class from the **S**hortcuts pull-down menu, or press Ctrl-L to access the Class List.

2. Use the Up and Down Arrow keys to move the arrow to the class that you want to edit.

3. Press Ctrl-E to access the Edit Class screen.

4. Make the necessary changes to the Edit Class screen.

5. Press Enter to save the changes.

Deleting a Class

You can delete classes from the Class List at any time. To delete a class, follow these steps:

1. Choose Select/Set Up Class from the **S**hortcuts pulldown menu, or press Ctrl-L to access the Class List.

2. Use the Up and Down Arrow keys to move the arrow to the class that you want to delete.

3. Press Ctrl-D to select the Delete option.

4. Quicken displays a warning that you are about to permanently delete a class.

5. Press Enter to delete the class.

Printing the Class List

You may want a hard copy of the classes that you have set up to use with Quicken. To print the Class List, follow these steps:

1. Choose Select/Set Up Class from the **S**hortcuts pulldown menu, or press Ctrl-L to access the Class list.

2. Press Ctrl-P to select the print option.

3. Type the number of the printer that you are using, if it is different than the default.

4. Press Enter to print the Class List.

Assigning Classes to Transactions

You can assign both a category and a class to a transaction, or just a class. To assign a class to a transaction:

1. Press Ctrl-R to access the check register as explained in Lesson 5. (Note: Classes can also be assigned to transactions from the Write Checks screen. See Lesson 12.)

2. Enter the transaction information such as date, check number, payee, payment or deposit amount, and memo.

3. If you are assigning a category and a class to the transaction, type the category name followed by a / in the Category field. If you are only assigning a class to the transaction, just type a /.

4. Type the class name after the forward slash. (Note: Quicken checks the class name that you enter to see if it is in the Class List. If not, Quicken gives you the option of selecting another class from the Class List or creating the new class that you just typed.)

5. Press Ctrl-Enter or F10 to record the transaction.

Assigning Classes Using the Class List

If you aren't sure which class you want to assign to a transaction, you can browse through the Class List and select the class directly from the list. To assign a class from the Class List, follow these steps:

1. With the highlight bar on the transaction, choose Select/ Set Up Class from the Shortcuts pull-down menu, or press Ctrl-L to access the Class list.

2. Use the Up and Down Arrow keys to look through the list.

3. Position the arrow on the class that you decide to assign to this transaction.

4. Press Enter.

5. Quicken enters the class name in the Category field.

6. Press Ctrl-Enter or F10 to record the transaction.

Setting Up Subclasses

Using subclasses in Quicken enables you to group and subtotal similar classes together. Quicken does not differentiate between classes and subclasses.

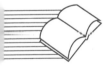

Subclass. A subclass provides even more detail for a transaction than a class provides. For example, if you have a category set up for clothing and a class set up for each family member, you might want to set up a subclass for the type of clothing. (For example, `Clothing/Jordan:Shoes`.)

Creating a Subclass

To create a subclass, refer to the previous section, "Creating Classes."

Assigning Subclasses to Transactions

To assign a subclass to a transaction, follow these steps:

1. Press Ctrl-R to access the check register, as explained in Lesson 5. (Note: Subclasses can also be assigned to transactions from the Write Checks screen. Refer to Lesson 12.)

2. Enter the transaction such as date, check number, payee, payment or deposit amount, and memo.

3. In the Category field, type the category name, a /, and the class name.

4. Type a : after the class name.

5. Type the subclass name after the colon. (Note: Quicken checks the subclass name that you enter to see if it is in the Class List. If not, Quicken gives you the option of selecting another subclass from the Class List or creating the new subclass that you just typed.)

6. Press Ctrl-Enter or F10 to record the transaction.

Assigning Subclasses Using the Class List

To assign a subclass using the Class List, follow the preceding steps for "Assigning Classes Using the Class List."

In this lesson you learned how to set up classes and subclasses and how to assign them to transactions. In the next lesson, you will learn how to memorize and recall transactions.

Lesson 10
Working with Memorized Transactions

In this lesson you will learn how to have Quicken memorize and recall transactions.

You can quickly record your transactions in the check register, the Write Checks screen (see Lesson 12), or any other Quicken account register by using Quicken to memorize the transaction and later recall the transaction.

A *memorized transaction* is saved information from one transaction to be recalled for later transactions. They are transactions that you frequently record to the same payee, in the same amount, or allocated to the same income or expense category. Paychecks, mortgage payments, and car loan payments are examples of transactions that you may want to memorize.

Memorizing a Transaction

To memorize a transaction, follow these steps:

1. Type the transaction information that you want to memorize. (Note: You can enter and memorize any part of a transaction; you do not have to memorize a complete transaction.)

2. Select **M**emorize Transaction from the **S**hortcuts pull-down menu or press Ctrl-M.

3. Quicken highlights the information and displays a message that the marked information is about to be memorized. Press Enter to memorize the transaction.

Memorizing Recorded Transactions. You can memorize transactions that have already been recorded in the register. Just highlight the transaction that you want to memorize and press Ctrl-M. Quicken memorizes the entire transaction except the date and the check number.

(Note: Quicken keeps two lists of memorized transactions; one for noninvestment accounts and one for investment accounts. You cannot recall a memorized, noninvestment account transaction to an investment account register and vice versa.)

Recalling a Memorized Transaction

Once you have memorized a transaction, you can recall the transaction and record it in the Write Checks screen or any Quicken register. To recall a memorized transaction:

1. At the Write Checks screen or in any Quicken account register, select **R**ecall Transaction from the **S**hortcuts pull-down menu or press Ctrl-T. (Note: If the transaction that you want to recall is a check to be printed, you must recall the transaction at the Write Checks screen.)

2. Quicken displays the Memorized Transactions List.

3. Scroll through the Memorized Transactions List (see Figure 10-1), using the Up and Down Arrow keys. Position the arrow on the transaction that you want to recall and press Enter.

4. To add information to the recalled transaction, continue typing information to complete the transaction.

5. Press Ctrl-Enter or F10 to record the transaction.

 **Recalling with Keystrokes**. To quickly recall a memorized transaction, type the first few letters of the payee name in the Payee field. Then press Ctrl-E. Quicken fills in the rest of the memorized transaction. If there is more than one payee in the Memorized Transactions List whose name begins with the same letters you typed, the Memorized Transaction List appears.

Memorized transaction

Type column indicates a payment, deposit, or check

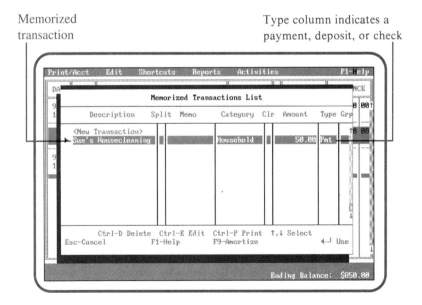

Figure 10-1. The Memorized Transactions List.

Adding a Transaction to the Memorized Transactions List

With Quicken 5 you can add a memorized transaction directly to the Memorized Transactions List. To add a memorized transaction, follow these steps:

1. Select **R**ecall Transaction from the **S**hortcuts pull-down menu or press Ctrl-T to access the Memorized Transactions List.

2. Press Home to highlight the <New Transaction> line.

3. Press Enter to access the Edit/Setup Memorized Transaction window shown in Figure 10-2.

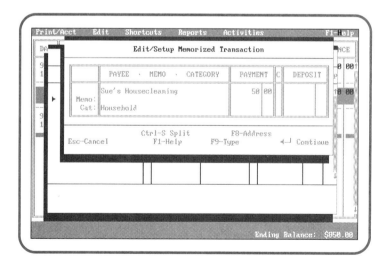

Figure 10-2. Adding a memorized transaction.

65

4. Type the transaction information in the Edit/Setup Memorized Transaction window. (Note: You can open the Split Transaction screen from this window to allocate the transaction to more than one category.)

5. Press F10 to add the transaction to the Memorized Transactions List.

Memorizing Addresses. From the Edit/Setup Memorized Transaction window, press F8 to memorize the address of the payee in a memorized transaction. Each time you recall the memorized transaction at the Write Checks screen, the memorized address will be filled in automatically.

Memorizing Deposit Transactions. From the Edit/Setup Memorized Transaction window, press F9 to designate a new memorized transaction as a deposit transaction. Quicken 5 allows you to memorize a deposit transaction with a 0.00 amount.

Editing a Memorized Transaction

You can edit memorized transactions directly from the Memorized Transactions List. To edit a memorized transaction, follow these steps:

1. Select **R**ecall Transaction from the **S**hortcuts pull-down menu or press Ctrl-T to access the Memorized Transactions List.

2. Use the Up and Down Arrow keys to highlight the memorized transaction that you want to edit.

3. Press Ctrl-E to access the Edit/Setup Memorized Transaction window.

4. Make the necessary changes to the memorized transaction and press F10.

Deleting a Memorized Transaction

At any time, you can delete a memorized transaction from the Memorized Transaction List. To delete a memorized transaction, follow these steps:

1. Select **R**ecall Transaction from the **S**hortcuts pull-down menu or press Ctrl-T to access the Memorized Transactions List.

2. Position the arrow on the memorized transaction from the Memorized Transaction List that you want to delete.

3. Press Ctrl-D to select the Delete option.

4. Quicken displays a message that you are about to delete a memorized transaction. Press Enter to delete the transaction.

Memorizing Loan Payments

With Quicken 5 you can memorize loan payments using the loan calculator. Each time you make a payment on a loan, Quicken records the principal and interest amounts from the amortization schedule generated by the loan calculator. To memorize a loan payment, follow these steps:

1. From the Write Checks screen or the check register, memorize a loan payment transaction as just explained.

2. Select **R**ecall Transaction from the **S**hortcuts pull-down menu or press Ctrl-T to access the Memorized Transactions List.

3. Highlight the memorized loan payment and press F9 to select the Amortize option.

4. Quicken displays the Set Amortization Information screen as shown in Figure 10-3.

Assign principal and interest categories to loan payment transactions

Quicken calculates the loan amount based on the payment, interest rate, total years, and periods entered

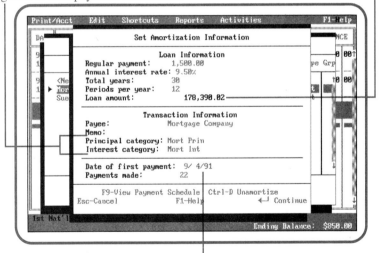

Enter the number of payments made on this loan to date

Figure 10-3. The Set Amortization Information screen to enter loan information.

5. In the Loan Information part of the screen, type the payment amount, annual interest rate, loan period (in

years), and the number of periods per year. Quicken calculates the approximate loan amount.

6. In the Transaction Information part of the screen, type the payee name, memo (optional), the category name to be assigned to the principal portion of the loan payment, and the category name to be assigned to the interest portion of the loan payment.

7. Type the date of the first loan payment and the number of payments made to date in the last part of the screen.

8. Press F9 to view the amortization schedule. Press Enter twice to memorize the loan payment and add it to the Memorized Transactions List. (Note: Memorized loan payments are designated by an A, for *amortized*, in the Split column of the Memorized Transactions List.)

Recording Memorized Loan Payments

When you are ready to make a payment on a loan that you have memorized, simply record the loan payment in the check register or the Write Checks screen. To record a memorized loan payment, follow these steps:

1. Select **R**ecall Transaction from the **S**hortcuts pull-down menu or press Ctrl-T to access the Memorized Transactions List.

2. Select the loan payment transaction.

3. Quicken records the loan payment and automatically applies the principal and interest amounts to the appropriate categories.

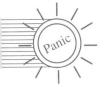

Canceling a Loan Payment. Each time you record a loan payment, Quicken increases the number of payments made on the loan by one. If you mistakenly record a loan payment, you must reset the number of payments made in the Payments Made field in the Set Amortization Information screen. After you reset the number of payments, you can delete the recorded payment from the check register.

Last Loan Payment. When you recall the last payment on a loan, Quicken reminds you that this is the last payment and will not let you recall this loan payment transaction again.

Printing the List

You may want a hard copy of the transactions that you have memorized. To print the Memorized Transaction List:

1. Select **R**ecall Transaction from the **S**hortcuts pull-down menu or press Ctrl-T to access the Memorized Transaction List.

2. Press Ctrl-P to select the Print option.

3. Type the number of the printer that you are using if it is different than the default.

4. Press Enter to print the Memorized Transaction List.

In this lesson you learned how to memorize and recall transactions. In the next lesson you will learn how to group transactions.

Lesson 11

Grouping Transactions

In this lesson you will learn how to set up and execute transaction groups.

Setting Up a Transaction Group

A *transaction group* is a group of recurring transactions that you pay or add to your account at the same time.

Transaction groups can have just one transaction or many. Quicken allows you to set up as many as 12 different transaction groups. Examples of transactions that you may want to set up in a transaction group are bills that are due at the beginning of the month, such as your mortgage payment, car loan payment, and insurance payment. To set up a transaction group, follow these steps:

1. Memorize the transactions that you want to include in the transaction group. (See Lesson 10.)

2. From the Write Checks screen or any account register, select Transaction Groups from the Shortcuts pull-down menu or press Ctrl-J to display the Select Transaction Group to Execute window, as in Figure 11-1.

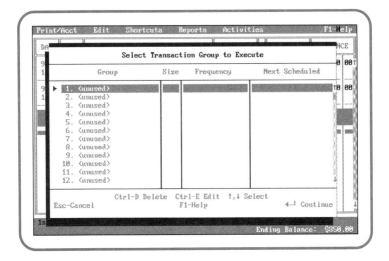

Figure 11-1. Select Transaction Group to Execute window.

3. Use the Up and Down Arrow keys to move the highlight bar to the first <unused> line and press Enter.

4. Quicken displays the Describe Group window as shown in Figure 11-2.

5. Type a descriptive name for the transaction group such as `Beg of month bills` and press Enter.

6. To automatically load an account before executing the transaction group, type the account name and press Enter. For example, if the transactions are associated with your Quicken checking account, type the account name (as it appears in the Select Account to Use window).

7. If the transaction group has a regular frequency and you want to schedule the group at specific intervals, type:

    2   Weekly

    3   Every two weeks

4	Twice a month
5	Every four weeks
6	Monthly
7	Quarterly
8	Twice a year
9	Annually

Otherwise, leave the frequency set at **1**. Press Enter.

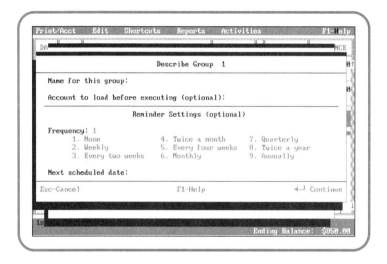

Figure 11-2. Describe Group window.

8. If you want to be reminded that the transactions in the transaction group are due, type the date that you first want to be reminded of transaction group due date. (Note: When a transaction group is due, Quicken will only remind you of the due date. Quicken will not execute or pay the transaction group automatically.)

9. Press Ctrl-Enter to record the information.

10. Quicken next displays the Assign Transactions to Group window (Figure 11-3). (Note: The transactions included in the Assign Transactions to Group window are transactions that you have previously memorized.)

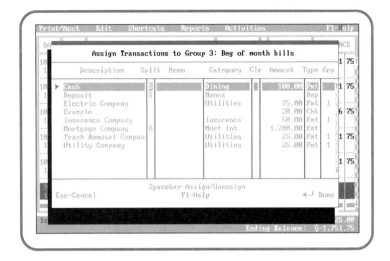

Figure 11-3. Assign Transactions to Group window.

11. Use the Up and Down Arrow keys to highlight each transaction to include in the transaction group.

12. Press the Spacebar to assign the highlighted transaction to the transaction group. The group number appears in the Grp column next to each transaction included in the transaction group. (Note: You can assign a transaction to more than one group.)

13. When you are finished assigning transactions, press Enter to set up the transaction group.

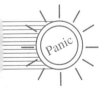

Transaction Groups for Printing Checks. To set up a transaction group for printing checks, be sure that you memorize transactions (for the transaction group) at the Write Checks screen. Transactions assigned at the Write Checks screen have the word Chk in the Type column of the Assign Transactions to Group window.

Adding a Transaction to a Transaction Group

You can add transactions to a transaction group at any time. To add a transaction to a transaction group:

1. From the Write Checks screen or any account register, select Transaction Groups from the Shortcuts pull-down menu or press Ctrl-J to display the Select Transaction Group to Execute window.

2. Use the Up and Down Arrow keys to highlight the transaction group to which you want to add a transaction.

3. Press Ctrl-E to access the Describe Group window.

4. Use Ctrl-Enter to show the list of memorized transactions.

5. Use the Up and Down Arrow keys to highlight the transaction you want to add to the transaction group.

6. Press the Spacebar to assign the highlighted transaction and press Enter to add the transaction.

Editing a Transaction Group

You can change the description or the assigned transactions in a transaction group at any time. To edit a transaction group, follow these steps:

1. From the Write Checks screen or any account register, select Transaction Groups from the Shortcuts pull-down menu or press Ctrl-J to display the Select Transaction Group to Execute window.

2. Use the Up and Down Arrow keys to highlight the transaction group that you want to edit.

3. Press Ctrl-E to access the Describe Group window.

4. To edit any of the information in the Describe Group window, make the changes and press Ctrl-Enter.

5. Quicken displays the Assign Transactions to Group window. To assign or unassign a transaction, use the Up and Down Arrow keys to highlight the transaction, then press the Spacebar.

6. Press Enter to save the changes to the transaction group.

Deleting a Transaction Group

To delete a transaction group, follow these steps:

1. From the Write Checks screen or any account register, select Transaction Groups from the Shortcuts pull-down menu or press Ctrl-J to display the Select Transaction Group to Execute window.

2. Use the Up and Down Arrow keys to highlight the transaction group that you want to delete.

3. Press Ctrl-D to select the Delete option.

4. Quicken displays the following:

   ```
   WARNING You are about to permanently delete a
   transaction group.
   ```

5. Press Enter to delete the transaction group.

Executing a Transaction Group

To record the transactions in a transaction group in the account register, you must execute the transaction group. When you do so, Quicken enters each transaction in the account register. Any changes to transactions can then be made from the register. To execute a transaction group:

1. From the Write Checks screen or any account register, select Transaction Groups from the Shortcuts pull-down menu or press Ctrl-J to display the Select Transaction Group to Execute window.

2. Use the Up and Down Arrow keys to highlight the transaction group you want to execute.

3. Quicken displays the Transaction Group Date window, showing the date that will be given to the transactions in the register.

4. Use the + or – keys to change the date if needed.

5. Quicken displays a message that the transactions from the group have been entered in the account register.

6. Press Enter.

Checks to be printed. If the transactions in the executed transaction group include checks that you want to print at this time, press Ctrl-W to display the Write Checks screen and then press Ctrl-P to print checks.

Lesson 12
Writing
Checks

In this lesson you will learn how to use Quicken to write checks.

Writing Checks

Checks that you want to print using Quicken are written at the Write Checks screen. Checks that you write are not printed until you tell Quicken to print checks. (See Lesson 13 to learn how to print checks).

The Write Checks screen is similar to a blank check. (Note: Checks written by hand are not entered in the Write Checks screen. Manual checks, deposits, and bank fees are entered in the check register. See Lesson 4 for more information on entering manual transactions.) To write a check in the Write Checks screen:

1. Select **Write/Print Checks** from the Main menu, or if you are at the check register, select **Write Checks** from the **Activities** pull-down menu or press Ctrl-W. Quicken displays the Write Checks screen as shown in Figure 12-1. (Note: Quicken checks are prenumbered so you do not enter a check number in this screen.)

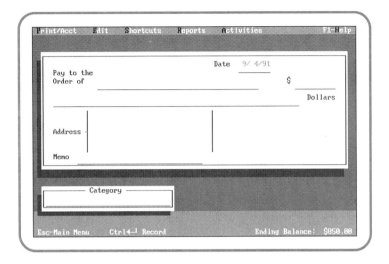

Figure 12-1. Writing a check at the Write Checks screen.

2. Type the date of the check and press Enter. (Note: Quicken automatically enters the current date; however, you can enter any date in the check's Date field.)

Changing Dates. To quickly change the date in the Write Checks screen, press + to increase the date one day at a time, or press – to decrease the date one day at a time

3. Type the payee's name and press Enter.

4. Type the amount of the check and press Enter. The maximum amount for any check is $9,999,999.99. Quicken automatically enters the written dollar amount.

5. If you are using window envelopes to mail your checks, type the payee's name and address and press Enter. You can enter up to five lines in the address field.

6. Type a memo for this check (optional) and press Enter.

7. If you want to assign a category, class, and/or subclass to this transaction, type the appropriate names in the Category field. (See Lessons 7, 8, and 9 for more on assigning categories and/or classes to transactions.)

8. Press Ctrl-Enter or F10 to record the check.

Memorized Transactions. If you write the same checks on a regular basis, you can memorize a check and recall it later so that you don't have to enter the same information each time. (See Lesson 10 to learn how to memorize a check.)

Writing Postdated Checks

You can write all of your checks at one time and type a future date (postdate) at the Write Checks screen. Then, as a postdated check becomes due, simply tell Quicken to print the check. Postdated checks appear in the check register with the date highlighted. Quicken calculates the total amount of unprinted checks so that you know exactly how much you will need to cover all postdated checks. The Checks to Print total appears in the lower right corner of the Write Checks screen.

Reviewing and Editing Checks

Before you print a check, you should review (and edit if necessary) the check that you have written. You can review and make changes to checks in the check register or at the Write Checks screen. To review and edit a check at the Write Checks screen, follow these steps:

1. Select **W**rite/Print Checks from the Main menu or if you are at the check register, select **W**rite Checks from the **A**ctivities pull-down menu or press Ctrl-W. Quicken displays the Write Checks screen.

2. Use the following keys to scroll through the checks at the Write Checks screen:

   PgUp to review the preceding check.

   PgDn to review the next check.

   Ctrl-Home to review the first check.

   Ctrl-End and PgUp to review the last check.

3. Review the check and make any necessary changes by typing over the entries in the Write Checks screen.

4. Press Ctrl-Enter to record the changes or Esc to cancel the changes.

5. Quicken automatically displays the next check.

Finding Checks. You can use the Find (Ctrl-F) and Go to Date (Ctrl-G) features of Quicken to locate a check. (See Lesson 5.)

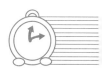

Deleting a Check

Checks that have been written but have not been printed can be deleted at any time. Checks can be deleted from the Write Checks screen or the check register. To delete a check from the Write Checks screen, follow these steps:

1. Select **W**rite/Print Checks from the Main menu; or if you are at the check register, select **W**rite Checks from the **A**ctivities pull-down menu or press Ctrl-W. Quicken displays the Write Checks screen.

2. Use the PgUp, PgDn, Ctrl-Home, or Ctrl-End keys to display the check that you want to delete.

3. Select **D**elete Transaction from the **E**dit pull-down menu or press Ctrl-D.

4. Quicken displays the OK to Delete Transaction window shown in Figure 12-2.

5. Press 1 to delete the check.

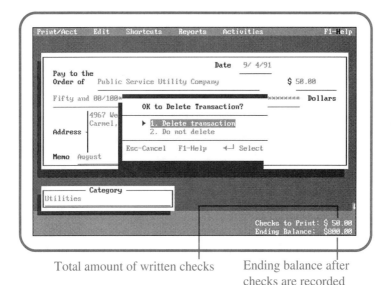

Total amount of written checks   Ending balance after checks are recorded

Figure 12-2. The OK to Delete Transaction window to delete a check.

Voiding a Check

You can *void* (cancel) a check that you have written using Quicken. Checks are voided in the check register, not the Write Checks screen. To void a check in the check register:

1. Press Ctrl-R to access the check register.

2. Use the Up and Down Arrow keys or the Find (Ctrl-F) and Go to Date (Ctrl-G) features to highlight the check that you want to void.

3. Select **V**oid Transaction from the **E**dit pull-down menu or press Ctrl-V.

4. Press 1 to void the transaction.

5. Quicken enters the word VOID before the payee name in the check register and marks the transaction with an X to show that it is cleared and should not be included in the next bank reconciliation.

In this lesson you learned how to write checks and how to edit, delete, and void checks written at the Write Checks screen. The next lesson will show you how to print checks.

Printing Checks

In this lesson you will learn how to print checks using Quicken.

Checks should be ordered from Intuit, publisher of Quicken, or any check printer that offers checks for use with Quicken. Quicken checks come in three different styles:

- Regular checks (3.5" high).
- Voucher checks (3.5" high, with a 3.5" perforated voucher below the check).
- Wallet checks (2 ^{5}/$_6$" high, with a stub on the left).

There are also two different check formats available:

- Continuous checks for use in continuous form printers.
- Laser checks that are grouped three to a page for regular checks, or one to a page for voucher checks.

Assigning Printer Settings

Before you can start printing checks, you must tell Quicken what kind of printer you are using by assigning printer settings, as follows:

1. Insert the sample checks into your printer (as you would continuous form paper) and turn on your printer.

2. Select **Write/Print** Checks from the Main menu or press Ctrl-W at the register to show the Write Checks screen.

3. Select **Print** Checks from the **Print**/Acct pull-down menu or just press Ctrl-P.

4. Quicken displays the Print Checks window. Type the number of the printer to print to and the number for the type of check that you are using.

5. Press F9 to print a sample check.

6. Review the sample check. If the sample check did not print correctly, type the position number to which the arrow for the *pointer line* (a mark that indicates where Quicken will start printing) is pointing and press Enter.

7. Quicken prints another sample check. Review the check. Repeat Step 6 as many times as necessary until the sample check prints correctly.

8. Press Enter when the sample check is printed correctly. Note the pointer line position and record it somewhere for future positioning.

   To position checks for use with a laser printer:

1. Insert the sample checks face down in your laser printer tray and turn on your printer.

2. Make sure that the Page-Oriented Printer setting in the Check Printer Settings window is set to Y. Refer to the previous section to learn how to change printer settings.

1. Select Set **P**references from the Main menu and then select **P**rinter Settings from the Set Preferences menu or just select Change Printer Styles from the **P**rint/Acct pull-down menu.

2. Press C to display the Style window.

3. Press Esc to remove the Style window and access the Select Check Printer List.

4. Use the Up and Down Arrow keys to highlight the name of your printer and press Enter to access the Style window for your printer.

5. Highlight the style of print that you want for your checks and press Enter.

6. Quicken displays the Check Printer Settings window.

7. Make any necessary changes to the Check Printer Settings window and press Enter.

Printer Settings. Quicken automatically enters the printer settings based on the printer that you select from the Printer List. Most of the time, these settings will be correct and no changes will be needed to the Check Printer Settings window.

Positioning Checks in Your Printer

You can use a continuous form printer or a laser printer to print your checks. Print sample checks first on blank paper to properly align checks before printing.

To position checks in a continuous form printer:

3. Select **W**rite/Print Checks from the Main menu or press Ctrl-W from the register to access the Write Checks screen.

4. Select **P**rint Checks from the **P**rint/Acct pull-down menu or just press Ctrl-P.

5. Quicken displays the Print Checks window. Type the number of the printer to print to and the number for the type of check that you are using and press Enter.

6. Press F9 to print a sample check.

7. Review the sample check. If the sample check did not print correctly, you may need to change printer settings.

Printing Checks

To print checks, follow these steps:

1. Turn on your printer and make sure that it is on-line.

2. Select **W**rite/Print Checks from the Main menu or press Ctrl-W from the register to access the Write Checks screen.

3. Select **P**rint Checks from the **P**rint/Acct pull-down menu or just press Ctrl-P.

4. Quicken displays the Print Checks window as shown in Figure 13-1.

5. Type the number of the printer that you want to use:

1 for Report Printer
2 for Alt Report Printer
3 for Check Printer

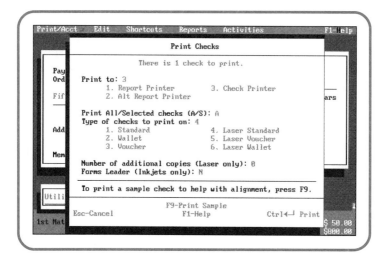

Figure 13-1. The Print Checks window.

6. Press Enter.

7. Tell Quicken which checks to print by pressing one of the following:

   A to print all checks
   S to print only selected checks

8. Type the number for the type of check that you are using and press Enter. (Note: You will not have to select the check type each time. Quicken will recall the check type the next time that you print checks.)

9. If you are using a laser printer, type the number of additional copies (up to three) that you want to print on a partial page of checks. (If you are using an inkjet printer, indicate whether you are using a laser forms leader.)

10. Press Enter.

11. If you typed an s to select the Selected Checks option in the Print Checks window, Quicken next displays the Select Checks to Print window shown in Figure 13-2. Use the Up and Down Arrow key to highlight each check that you want to print and press Spacebar to select/deselect a check to print or press F9 to select all checks. Press Enter when you have selected the checks.

12. At the Enter Check Number window, type the next blank check number if the number shown is not correct.

Changing Check Numbers. To quickly change the check number in the Enter Check Number window, press + to increase the check number or – to decrease the check number.

13. Press Enter to begin printing checks. (Quicken will ask you if your check(s) printed correctly. Press 1 for Yes and 2 for No.)

Incorrectly Printed Checks. Be sure to review all printed checks before you mail them. If a check is incorrect, you may reprint the check as explained in the next section.

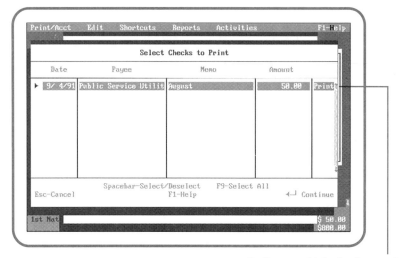

Indicates which checks to print

Figure 13-2. The Select Checks to Print window displays which checks you want printed.

Reprinting Checks

You can reprint a check at any time. To reprint a check:

1. Press Ctrl-R to access the check register.

2. Locate the check that you want to reprint.

3. Type an asterisk (*) in the Num (Check Number) field. Quicken changes the entry to a row of asterisks.

4. Press Ctrl-Enter or F10 to record the change to the Num field.

5. Press Ctrl-W to access the Write Checks screen.

6. Print the check by following the steps for printing selected checks.

Lesson 14

Reconciling Your Bank Account

In this lesson you will learn how to reconcile your bank account to your Quicken check register.

A bank reconciliation is a procedure to compare the balance shown on your bank statement at the end of a specific period to the balance shown in the check register at the end of the same period. You should reconcile your account with your bank statement each time you receive a statement to ensure:

- You successfully recorded the same transactions that the bank statement shows.

- Your recorded transactions are accurate.

- The bank statement correctly reflects your transactions for the period. (Banks sometimes make mistakes!)

Entering Information from Your Bank Statement

You must enter the information shown on your bank statement in Quicken before you can reconcile your bank account. To enter information from your bank statement:

1. Press Ctrl-R from the Main menu to access the check register. Make sure that the register you access is the register for the bank account you are reconciling.

2. Select **R**econcile from the **A**ctivities pull-down menu.

3. Quicken displays the Reconcile Register with Bank Statement window shown in Figure 14-1. Compare the opening balance shown in the window with the opening balance shown on your statement. If this is the first time you have reconciled your account, there may be a difference in the Bank Statement Opening Balance field. If necessary, type the correct opening balance and press Enter.

Figure 14-1. The Reconcile Register with Bank Statement window.

4. Type the ending balance on your bank statement and press Enter.

5. Type any transactions to be added: service charges and interest earned, and a category name to allocate the transactions, if desired. (Note: If you want to see your last reconciliation report, press F9 from the Reconcile Register with Bank Statement window to print a copy.)

6. Press Ctrl-Enter to record the information in the Reconcile Register with Bank Statement window.

7. Quicken next displays a list of uncleared transactions and a Reconciliation Summary.

Marking Cleared Transactions

The next step in reconciling your bank account is to mark all of the cleared transactions in the check register.

Cleared Transactions. Cleared transactions are transactions that are recorded in the check register and *have been* processed by the bank. Cleared transactions may include deposits, checks (withdrawals), ATM transactions, and so on.

To mark cleared transactions, follow these steps:

1. From the list of uncleared transactions (see Figure 14-2) displayed after information is entered in the Reconcile Register with Bank Statement window, use the Up and Down Arrow keys to highlight each transaction that appears on your bank statement.

2. For each transaction highlighted, press Enter to mark the transaction as cleared. Quicken will enter an asterisk in the Clear column (the column next to the Check Number column) to show that the transaction has cleared.

To unmark a transaction, highlight the transaction and press the Spacebar.

Check Number Column   Clear Column

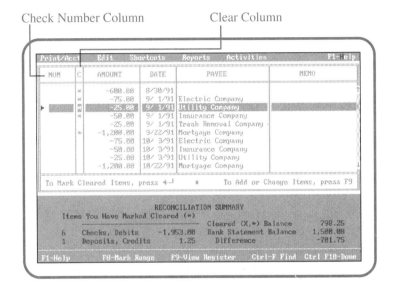

Figure 14-2. Marking cleared transactions.

Marking Transactions. To quickly move through the list of transactions with your left hand (use your right hand to check off transactions on your bank statement), use the F5 and F6 keys to move the highlight bar up and down.

Marking a Range of Cleared Checks

If an uninterrupted sequence of checks appears on your bank statement as cleared, you can mark the range as cleared without marking each individual check. To mark a range of cleared checks, follow these steps:

1. Press F8 to display the Mark Range of Check Numbers as Cleared window shown in Figure 14-3.

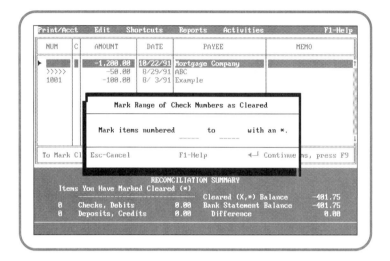

Figure 14-3. The Mark Range of Check Numbers as Cleared window.

2. Type the beginning and ending check numbers for the range of checks that you want to mark as cleared and press Enter.

3. Quicken marks (with asterisks) all of the checks within the specified range as cleared.

Completing the Bank Reconciliation

The reconciliation can be completed after you have marked all cleared transactions. To complete the bank reconciliation, follow these steps:

1. Review the RECONCILIATION SUMMARY at the bottom of the uncleared transactions list. If the difference is zero, then your bank account balances and you may complete the reconciliation. If the difference is a value other than zero, (see the next section) then you need to either find the difference or have Quicken adjust your check register balance to agree with the bank statement balance.

2. If your bank account balances, then press Ctrl-F10 from the uncleared transactions list to have Quicken reconcile your account.

3. Quicken displays a congratulatory message and asks if you want to print a Reconciliation Report.

4. If you want to print the report, type Y and then press Enter. (Note: You do not have to print the Reconciliation Report to complete the bank reconciliation.)

5. Quicken displays the Print Reconciliation Report window. Type the number of the printer to send the report to and press Enter.

6. Type a reconcile date if you want the date on the report to be a date other than the current date. Press Enter.

7. If you want a detailed report, change the S to F and press Enter.

8. Type a report title, if desired.

9. Press Ctrl-Enter to print the report.

Adjusting for Differences

If the difference shown in the Reconciliation Summary is a value other than zero, then you can go back through the transactions to try to locate the difference, or have Quicken make an adjustment in your check register for the difference. To have Quicken adjust the difference:

1. Press Ctrl-F10 from the uncleared transactions list to have Quicken reconcile your account.

2. If the difference is due to a discrepancy between the opening balance in your account and the opening balance on your statement, Quicken asks if you want to create a balance adjustment. Type Y to create the adjustment or N to complete the reconciliation without adjusting the register balance.

3. If the difference results from the transactions during the period, Quicken displays the Adding Balance Adjustment Entry window.

4. Quicken tells you what the adjusting entry will be and asks if you want to add it to the register. Type Y to add the adjustment to the register and type a category name (optional) for this transaction.

5. Press Enter to create the adjusting entry.

Deleting Adjusting Entries. Adjusting entries can be deleted from the check register if you later find the error that resulted in the reconciliation difference.

In the next lesson you will learn how to set up and use a credit card account.

Working with Credit Card Accounts

In this lesson you will learn how to set up a credit card account that you can use to track your credit card transactions.

If you pay your credit card bills on a current basis (pay the balance each month), you probably do not need to set up a credit card account. You can enter credit card transactions in the check register when you pay your credit card bill and split the transaction so that you can assign a separate category to each transaction. However, if you do not pay your credit card bill on a current basis, you should set up a credit card account to track your credit card purchases and payments.

Credit Card Account. A credit card account is a Quicken account used to enter credit card purchases and payments. A separate account should be set up for each of your credit card accounts. You can set up a credit card account for MasterCard, Visa, Discover, etc.

Setting Up a Credit Card Account

To set up a credit card account, refer to Lesson 3 for an explanation on setting up a new account. Go to the Set Up New Account screen (see Figure 3-2) and follow these steps:

1. Press 2 to select Credit Card in the Account Type field in the Set Up New Account screen. Press Enter.

2. Type the name of the credit card account and press Enter.

3. Type the starting balance in the credit card account and press Enter. This is the account balance as of the date that you specify (in the next step) as the start date.

4. Type the date that relates to the starting balance you entered in Step 3 and press Enter. If you are using your last credit card statement balance, enter the statement date.

5. Type a description (optional) of the account and press Enter. It is useful to enter the credit card account number here.

6. Quicken displays the Specify Credit Limit window. Type the credit limit that applies to this credit card account (optional).

7. Press Enter to add the credit card account to the Quicken account list.

Entering Transactions in the Credit Card Register

Enter credit card purchases and finance charges in the credit card register throughout the month as you make purchases, or at the end of the month when you receive your monthly statement. To enter transactions in the credit card register, follow these steps:

1. Choose Select Account from the Main menu to display the Select Account to Use window or, from the Write Checks screen or any register, press Ctrl-A.

2. Use the Up and Down Arrow keys to highlight the credit card account that you want to use and press Enter.

3. Quicken displays the credit card register (see Figure 15-1) for the account that you selected. (Note: The credit card register resembles the check register.)

4. Enter transactions the same way they are entered in the check register. (Refer to Lesson 5.)

Entering Transactions. You can memorize and recall transactions in the credit card register. (Refer to Lesson 10.) You can also split transactions in the credit card register. (Refer to Lesson 8.)

Marking Cleared Credit Card Transactions. If you enter credit card purchases from your monthly statement, type an asterisk (*) in the C (Clear) column when you enter the transaction. This will save you time when you reconcile your credit card account.

Amount charged   Amount paid

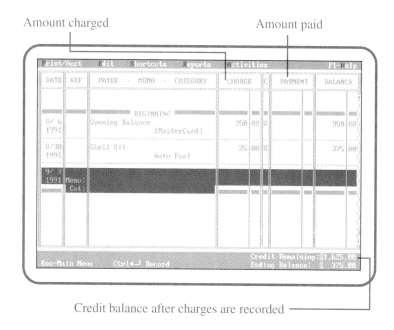

Credit balance after charges are recorded

Figure 15-1. The credit card register.

Reconciling and Paying Your Credit Card Account

Quicken reconciles your credit card account and creates a transaction for any expenses that are shown on your credit card statement but are not reflected in the credit card register, such as finance charges or credit card fees. Quicken then gives you the option of paying the credit card company through a handwritten check or a Quicken check. To reconcile and pay your credit card account, follow these steps:

1. From the credit card register, select the **R**econcile/Pay Credit Card option from the **A**ctivities pull-down menu.

101

2. Quicken displays the Credit Card Statement Information window as shown in Figure 15-2.

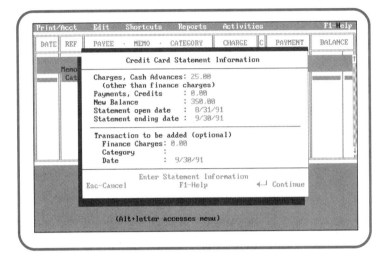

Figure 15-2. The Credit Card Statement Information window for entering information from your monthly statement.

3. Type charges, cash advances, payments, credits, the new balance, and the opening and ending dates from your credit card statement and press Enter.

4. Type finance charges (optional) and a category name to allocate finance charges.

5. Press Enter to display the uncleared transactions list as shown in Figure 15-3.

6. Use the Up and Down Arrow keys to highlight each transaction that appears on your credit card statement. For each transaction highlighted, press the Enter key to mark the transaction as cleared. Quicken will enter an

asterisk in the column next to the Reference column to show that the transaction has cleared. (Note: In the last lesson you learned how to mark a range of transactions as cleared. You can also mark ranges of transactions in the credit card register.)

Clear column

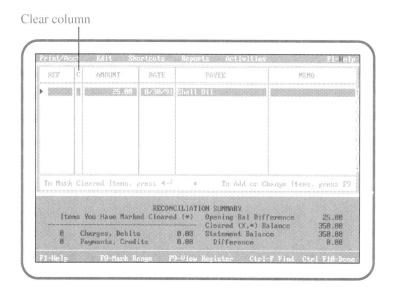

Figure 15-3. Marking cleared transactions from the uncleared transactions list.

Switching to the Credit Card Register. If you need to go back to the credit card register while you are marking transactions in the uncleared transactions list, press F9. Press F9 again to go back to the uncleared transactions list.

7. Press Ctrl-F10 when you are finished marking cleared transactions.

8. Review the Reconciliation Summary at the bottom of the uncleared transactions list. If the difference is zero, then your credit card account balances, and you may go on to Step 9 and complete the reconciliation. If the difference is a value other than zero, then you need to either find the difference (press Esc) or have Quicken adjust your credit card register balance to agree with your credit card statement (press Enter at the Adjusting Register to Agree with Statement window).

9. If your credit card account balances, Quicken displays the Make Credit Card Payment window.

10. Type the name of the checking account (or press Ctrl-C for a listing of accounts) to use to pay the credit card bill and press Enter.

11. Type y to make out a Quicken check, or type n to make out a handwritten check.

12. Press Enter to process and record the payment in the check register and in the credit card register, or press Esc if you do not want to pay the credit card bill now.

Transferring Funds to Your Credit Card Account

When you pay your credit card bill, you can automatically transfer funds from your bank account to your credit card account. To transfer funds to your credit card account, follow these steps:

1. From the Write Checks screen or the check register, enter the payment to the credit card company.

2. In the Category field, type the name of the credit card account to which you want the funds (or payment) transferred. Quicken enters the name of the credit card account enclosed in brackets to indicate a transfer.

3. Press Ctrl-Enter to record the payment.

4. Quicken enters the payment amount as a PAYMENT to your credit card account and decreases the outstanding balance by the amount of the payment.

Transferring Funds from Your Credit Card Account

If your credit card account provides for cash advances or overdraft protection for your bank account, you can transfer funds from your credit card account to your bank account. To transfer funds from your credit card account, follow these steps:

1. From the credit card register, enter the charge to your credit card account.

2. In the Category field, type the name of the bank account that you want the funds transferred to. Quicken enters the name of the bank account enclosed in brackets to indicate a transfer.

3. Press Ctrl-Enter to record the charge.

4. Quicken enters the charge amount as a DEPOSIT to your bank account and increases the outstanding balance by the amount of the charge.

In the next lesson, you will learn how to set up and use a cash account.

Lesson 16

Working with Cash Accounts

In this lesson you will learn how to set up a cash account that you can use to keep track of your cash expenditures.

A *cash account* is a Quicken account used to track cash transactions. Cash accounts should be used if you prefer to use cash instead of checks or credit cards, if you normally get paid in cash, or in the case of a business, if you must track petty cash.

Setting Up a Cash Account

To set up a cash account, refer to Lesson 3 for an explanation on setting up a new account. Go to the Set Up New Account screen (see Figure 3-2) and follow these steps:

1. Press 3 to select Cash in the Account Type field in the Set Up New Account screen and press Enter.

2. Type the name of the cash account and press Enter.

3. Type the starting balance in the cash account and press Enter. This is the amount of cash on hand as of the date that you specify (in the next step) as the start date.

4. Type the date that relates to the starting balance entered in Step 3 and press Enter.

5. Type a description (optional) of the account.

6. Press Enter to add the cash account to the Quicken account list.

Entering Cash Transactions in the Check Register

If you have a bank account set up, you can enter cash transactions directly into the check register. (See Lesson 5 to enter cash transactions in the check register.)

Entering Cash Transactions in the Cash Register

To enter cash transactions in the cash register, follow these steps:

1. Choose Select Account from the Main menu to display the Select Account to Use window.

2. Use the Up and Down Arrow keys to highlight the cash account and press Enter.

3. Quicken displays the cash register shown in Figure 16-1. (Note: The cash register resembles the check register.)

4. Enter transactions the same way as they are entered in the check register (see Lesson 5).

Cash spent   Cash received

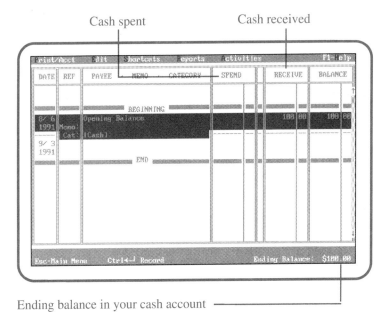

Ending balance in your cash account

Figure 16-1. The cash register.

Entering Cash Transactions. You can memorize and recall transactions in the cash register (see Lesson 10). You can also split transactions in the cash register (see Lesson 8).

Transferring Funds to Your Cash Account

With just one transaction, funds can be withdrawn from your Quicken bank account to your cash account. To transfer funds to your cash account, follow these steps:

1. From the Write Checks screen or the check register, enter the transaction for the cash of your check or withdrawal.

2. In the Category field, type the name of the cash account to which you want the funds transferred. Quicken enters the name of the cash account enclosed in brackets to indicate a transfer.

3. Press Ctrl-Enter to record the transfer.

4. Quicken records the cash amount as a RECEIVE entry in the cash account and increases the cash balance by the amount of the transfer.

Updating Your Cash Account Balance

Reconciliations are performed on bank accounts and credit card accounts. Although it is not necessary to perform a reconciliation on a cash account, you should periodically update your cash account balance to accurately reflect your cash on hand. To update your cash account balance, follow these steps:

1. From the cash register, select Update Account Balances from the Activities pull-down menu.

2. Quicken displays the Update Account Balance window shown in Figure 16-2.

3. Type the amount of cash on hand and press Enter.

4. Type the category name (optional) for this adjusting transaction.

109

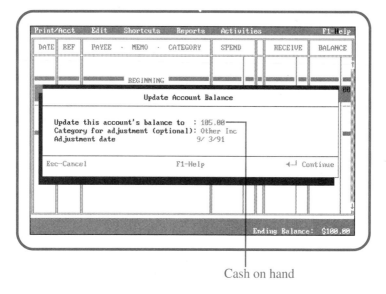

Cash on hand

Figure 16-2. The Update Account Balance window.

5. Press Enter to update your cash account balance. If the amount of cash that you entered is more than the cash account balance, Quicken enters an adjustment in the RECEIVE column of the cash register. If the amount of cash that you entered is less than the cash account balance, Quicken enters an adjustment in the SPEND column of the cash register.

In this lesson you learned how to set up and use a cash account. In the next lesson, you will learn how to work with asset and liability accounts.

Working with Other Asset and Other Liability Accounts

In this lesson you will learn how to set up and use other asset and other liability accounts.

An *other asset account* is a Quicken account used to track the things that you own. Examples of assets that you may want to set up a separate account for are your home, 401K account, and your automobile. In the case of a business, you can set up an other asset account for accounts receivable, capital equipment, and real estate.

An *other liability account* is a Quicken account used to track the debts that you owe. Examples of liabilities that you may want to set up a separate account for are your home mortgage, car loans, and any other type of loan. Business users can set up an other liability account for accrued payroll and income taxes.

Setting Up Other Asset and Other Liability Accounts

To set up other asset and other liability accounts, refer to Lesson 3 for an explanation on setting up a new account. Go to the Set Up New Account screen (see Figure 3-2) and follow these steps:

1. Press 4 to select Other Asset, or press 5 to select Other Liability in the Account Type field in the Set Up New Account screen and press Enter.

2. Type the name of the other asset or other liability account and press Enter.

3. Type the starting balance in the other asset or other liability account and press Enter. For an other asset account, this is the value of the asset as of the date that you specify (in the next step) as the start date. For an other liability account, this is the amount that you owe as of the date that you specify (in the next step) as the start date.

4. Type the date that relates to the starting balance that you entered in Step 3 and press Enter.

5. Type a description (optional) of the other asset or other liability account.

6. Press Enter to add the other asset or other liability account to the Quicken account list.

Entering Transactions in Other Asset and Other Liability Accounts

Transactions that affect other asset and other liability accounts can be entered directly in the other asset and other liability registers. For example, to record the increase in value of an other asset account, you should enter the increase in the other asset register (see Figure 17-1).

Some transactions can be entered into other accounts, such as a bank account, and transferred to an other asset or other liability account. For example, if you write a check for home improvements, you can enter the transaction in the Write Checks screen for your bank account and transfer the transaction to the other asset account that you have set up for your home.

Entering Transactions in Other Asset and Other Liability Registers

To enter a transaction in an other asset or other liability register, follow these steps:

1. Choose Select Account from the Main menu to display the Select Account to Use window.

2. Use the Up and Down Arrow keys to highlight the other asset or other liability account that you want to use.

3. Press Enter to access the other asset or other liability register. The other asset register (see Figure 17-1), resembles the check register, as does the other liability register shown in Figure 17-2.

4. Enter transactions the same way they are entered in the check register (see Lesson 5).

5. Press Ctrl-Enter or F10 to record the transactions in the other asset or other liability registers.

Recording Transactions from Other Accounts

To record transactions from other accounts to an other asset or other liability account, follow these steps:

1. Access the register for the other account, such as a bank account.

Entries in the Decrease Column decrease the value of the asset

Entries in the Increase Column add to the value of the asset

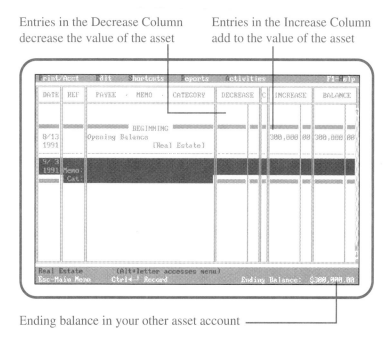

Ending balance in your other asset account

Figure 17-1. The other asset register to record transactions.

2. Enter the transaction as you would any other transaction.

3. In the Category field of the account register, type the name of the other asset or other liability account to which you want to transfer the transaction. Quicken enters the name of the other asset or other liability account enclosed in brackets to indicate a transfer.

4. Press Ctrl-Enter to record the transfer. Quicken records an INCREASE or a DECREASE in the other asset or other liability account.

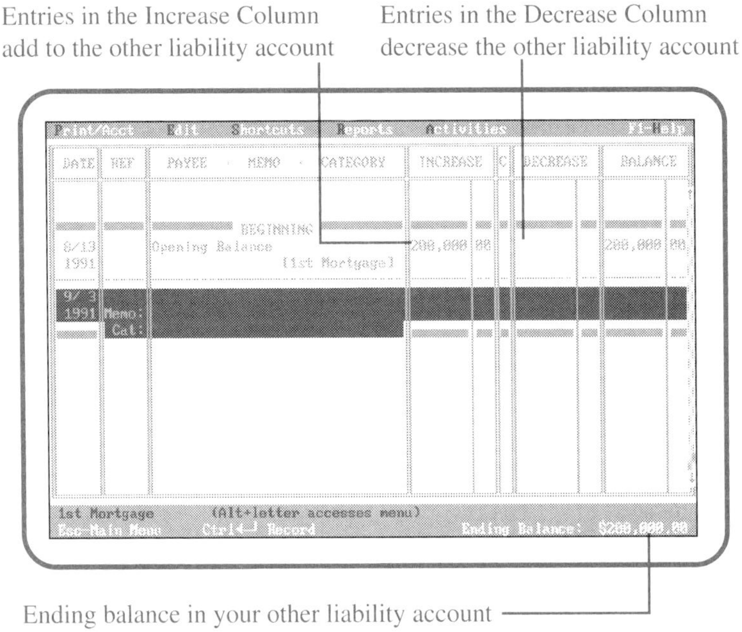

Entries in the Increase Column add to the other liability account

Entries in the Decrease Column decrease the other liability account

Ending balance in your other liability account

Figure 17-2. The other liability register to record transactions.

Updating Other Asset and Other Liability Account Balances

Reconciliations are performed on bank accounts and credit card accounts. Although it is not necessary to perform a reconciliation on an other asset or other liability account, you should periodically update your other asset and other liability account balances to accurately reflect the value of your assets and liabilities. To update your other asset and other liability account balances, follow these steps:

1. At the other asset or other liability register, select **U**pdate Account Balances from the **A**ctivities pull-down menu.

115

2. Quicken displays the Update Account Balance window shown in Figure 17-3.

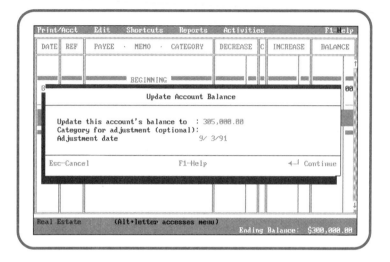

Figure 17-3. The Update Account Balance window.

3. Type the current value of the account and press Enter.

4. Type the category name (optional) for this adjusting transaction.

5. Press Enter to update your other asset or other liability account balance. If the value of assets or liabilities that you entered is more than the account balance, Quicken enters an adjustment in the INCREASE column of the register. If the value of assets or liabilities that you entered is less than the account balance, Quicken enters an adjustment in the DECREASE column of the register.

In this lesson you learned how to set up and work with other asset and other liability accounts. In the next lesson, you will learn how to work with investment accounts.

Creating and Printing Reports

In this lesson you will learn how to create and print Quicken's standard reports.

The Quicken program includes preset reports that can be viewed on your screen or printed. Preset reports consist of 7 personal reports, 8 business reports, and 5 investment reports. In addition, Quicken allows you to create your own custom reports or customize any of the preset reports. (See Lesson 20 for an explanation on customizing reports.)

Creating Reports

To create reports, follow these steps:

1. Select Create Reports from the Main menu or Alt-R from any register or the Write Checks screen. Quicken displays the Reports menu.

2. Select one of the following options:

   Personal Reports

   Business Reports

   Investment Reports

3. A different list of reports is displayed, dependent on your selection made in Step 2. For example, if you selected Personal Reports, Quicken displays a list of seven reports (see Figure 18-1) that you can create for your personal needs.

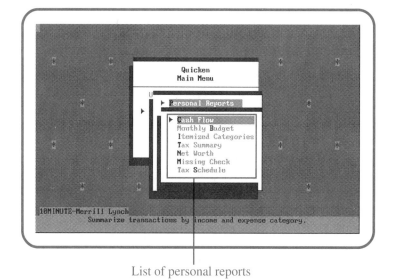

List of personal reports

Figure 18-1. The list of personal reports.

4. Select the report that you want to create to display the report window. Figure 18-2 shows the Cash Flow Report window.

5. Type a report title (optional) and the date(s) that the report is to cover. (Note: The report window for investment reports requires additional information such as how to subtotal the report and whether to include current, all, or selected investment accounts in the report.) When you have finished filling in the report window, press Ctrl-Enter to create the report. Quicken searches through the transactions and displays the report on your screen.

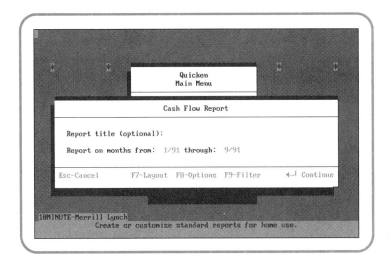

Figure 18-2. The Cash Flow Report window.

Printing Reports

Reports that you have created can be printed. However, before printing reports, you must assign printer settings in Quicken.

To assign printer settings in Quicken, refer to Lesson 13. To assign printer settings for reports, use the same procedure but select Report Printer Settings instead from the Printer Settings menu.

To print reports, follow these steps:

1. Position paper in your printer and turn it on.

2. With the report displayed on your screen, select **P**rint Report from the **F**ile/Print pull-down menu or simply press Ctrl-P.

119

3. Quicken displays the Print Report window shown in Figure 18-3.

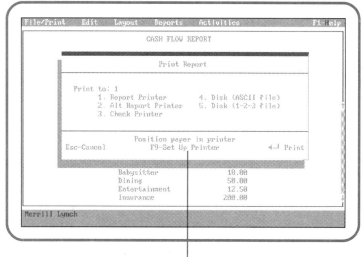

Press F9 to select printer settings (if you haven't already done so)

Figure 18-3. The Print Report window for printing a report.

4. Type the number of the printer to which you want to send the report. Type 1 for the report printer that you set up. If you want the report sent to the alternate report printer, type 2.

5. Press Enter to send the report to your printer.

Changing Printer Settings. If you need to change the printer settings that are shown in the Print Report window, press F9 from the Print Report window. Quicken allows you to change the printer settings while the report is still on your screen.

Lesson 19

Using Other Report Features

In this lesson you will learn how to further customize your Quicken reports.

Moving Around the Report Screen

When a report is on-screen, you may need to move around the report screen to examine the detail behind a report entry or to view another entry. To move around the report:

Press	To Move
Tab or Right Arrow	One column to the right
Shift-Tab or Left Arrow	One column to the left
Ctrl-Right Arrow	One screen to the right
Ctrl-Left Arrow	One screen to the left
PgUp and PgDn	Up or down one screen
Home	To the far left, current row
End	To the far right, current row
Home-Home	To the top left corner of the report
End-End	To the bottom right corner of the report

Editing Reports in the Report Screen

Quicken 5 now has the capability to edit reports while they are on your screen through the use of pull-down menus. With the report on-screen, you can do the following:

- Print and memorize reports
- Examine (QuickZoom) report detail
- Set titles and date ranges
- Filter transactions, accounts, categories, and classes
- Change the layout of the report
- Collapse or expand report detail

With the exception of the QuickZoom, Collapse, and Expand features, all report editing features are explained in Lesson 20.

Using QuickZoom

Another new feature in Quicken 5 is QuickZoom which allows you to examine the transaction detail behind a report entry. (Note: This feature can only be used with noninvestment summary reports and budget reports.) To use QuickZoom, follow these steps:

1. With the report displayed on your screen, move the cursor to the report entry that you want to examine.

2. Select QuickZoom from the File/Print pull-down menu or just press Ctrl-Z. If you are using a mouse, double-click on the report entry.

3. For summary or budget reports, Quicken displays a Transaction List window (Figure19-1). For transaction reports, it displays the register entry for the report entry.

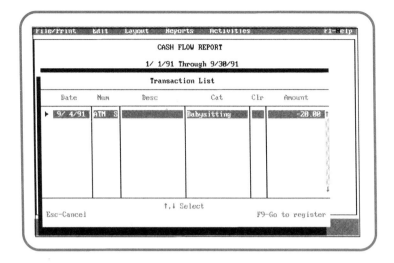

Figure 19-1. The Transaction List window listing the transaction detail behind a report entry.

4. To display the register entry for a transaction listed in the Transaction List window, move the cursor to the transaction and press F9. (Note: You cannot return to the report screen from the register screen.)

Using the Collapse Feature

The collapse feature, also new in Quicken 5, allows you to summarize the detail for a row heading in summary, budget, or account balance reports without changing the report totals. For example, if you want to present Total Inflows in a Cash Flow Report as just one line in the report, you can collapse the row heading and Quicken reduces the Total Inflows section of the report to a single line. (Note: You cannot use the collapse feature with transaction reports.) To collapse a row heading:

1. With the report displayed on your screen, position the cursor on the row heading that you want to summarize or collapse. Figure 19-2 shows a report before collapsing a row heading.

2. Select **Collapse** from the **Layout** pull-down menu or double-click on the row heading.

3. Quicken now displays one line for the row heading, as shown in Figure 19-3.

(Note: When you collapse a category within a section of a report, Quicken moves the category to the end of the section and then removes the *category* title and replaces it with a *hidden* title. For example, if you collapse the Salary Income category in the Inflows section of a cash flow report, Quicken moves the category to the end of the Inflows section and replaces the Salary Income title with the title Inflows - Hidden.)

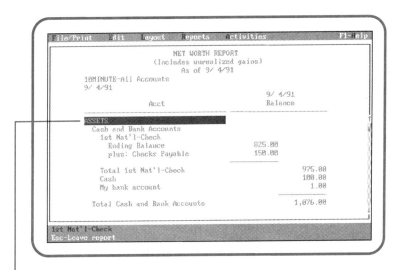

Row reading before Collapse *lists* all of the details in that report section.

Figure 19-2. A sample report that shows a row heading before it has been collapsed.

The collapsed reading summarizes all the entries in that report section

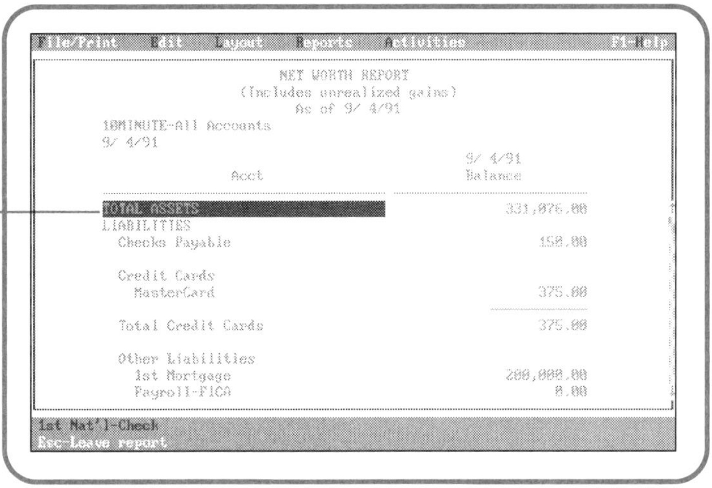

Figure 19-3. A sample report that shows a row heading after it has been collapsed.

Expanding Report Detail

Return any detail in a report that is summarized or collapsed to its original format with the Expand feature. To expand report detail:

1. Place the cursor on the row heading you want to expand.

2. Select **E**xpand from the **L**ayout pull-down menu or double-click on the row heading.

3. Quicken displays the detail for the row heading.

In the next lesson you will learn how to customize reports.

Customizing Reports

In this lesson you will learn how to create your own custom reports or customize any one of Quicken's preset reports.

Creating Custom Reports

You can create four unique forms of custom reports; transaction, summary, budget, and account balance reports. Creating custom reports allows you to do the following:

- Sort and subtotal transactions
- Subtotal categories, classes, and payees
- Compare actual income and expenses to a budget
- List the balances from all accounts in the current account file to determine your net worth

You can also choose how reports are organized and which transactions are included in reports. To create a custom report, follow these steps:

1. Select Create Reports from the Main menu or press Alt-R from any register or the Write Checks screen. Quicken displays the Reports menu.

2. Select one of the following reports:

Transaction
Summary
Budget
Account Balances

A different create report window is displayed, dependent on your selection in Step 2. For example, if you selected Transaction Reports, Quicken displays the Create Transaction Report window (Figure 20-1).

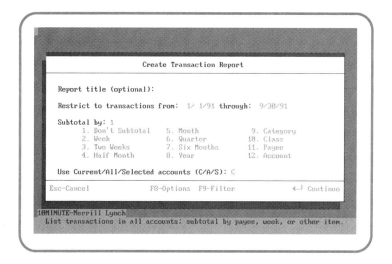

```
                    Create Transaction Report

Report title (optional):

Restrict to transactions from:  1/ 1/91 through:  9/30/91

Subtotal by: 1
       1. Don't Subtotal    5. Month          9. Category
       2. Week              6. Quarter        10. Class
       3. Two Weeks         7. Six Months     11. Payee
       4. Half Month        8. Year           12. Account

Use Current/All/Selected accounts (C/A/S): C

Esc-Cancel              F8-Options  F9-Filter          ←┘ Continue

10MINUTE-Merrill Lynch
   List transactions in all accounts; subtotal by payee, week, or other item.
```

Figure 20-1. The Create Transaction Report window.

3. At the create report window, type a report title (optional), and the date(s) that the report is to cover.

For *transaction reports*, type the number that corresponds to the method for subtotaling the report.

For *summary reports*, type the number that corresponds to headings for report rows and columns.

For *budget reports*, type the number that corresponds to the column headings of the report.

For *account balances reports*, type the number that corresponds to the intervals for balances to be reported.

4. For all reports, type c to include data from only the current account (displayed in the bottom-left corner of the create report window), type A to include data from all accounts in the account files, or type s to include data from only selected accounts.

5. To set report options, press F8 or to filter report transactions, press F9.

6. At the create report window, press Ctrl-Enter. If you typed s (Selected Accounts) in the last field of the create report window, Quicken displays a list of accounts. To select an account to include, position the arrow on an account and press the Spacebar. Continue selecting accounts and press Enter. (Note: For account balances reports, you can press the Spacebar to select the Detail option for an account, which shows the class or security detail behind an account.) Quicken displays the report on your screen.

Setting Report Options

Setting report options allows you to choose how the report is organized, how transfers are handled, and how dollars and cents and subcategories are displayed. For transaction reports, you can choose how totals, split transactions, memos, and categories are displayed. To set report options:

1. From any create report window, press F8 to display the Report Options window shown in Figure 20-2.

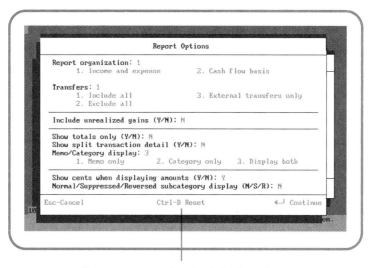

Resets report option the default settings

Figure 20-2. The Report Options window customizes reports.

2. Fill in the Report Options window and press Enter to return to the Create Report window. If you want to reset the report, press Ctrl-D at the Report Options window.

Changing Report Layout. Once you have created and displayed a report on-screen, you can change the report layout using the options on the **L**ayout pull-down menu (Alt-L).

Customizing Preset Reports

Quicken allows you to customize its preset Personal, Business, and Investment reports. To customize preset reports:

1. From the report window (displayed after you select a report to create from the list of reports), press F8 to display the Report Options window as in Figure 21-2.

2. Fill in the Report Options window and press Enter to return to the Create Report window. If you want to reset the report, press Ctrl-D at the Report Options window.

Memorizing Reports

You can memorize regularly used reports so that you can access them quickly. To memorize reports:

1. From the Report window or the Create Report window, press Ctrl-M to display the Memorize Report window.

2. Type a report title, if desired. Press Enter.

Accessing Memorized Reports

To access a memorized report, follow these steps:

1. Select Memorized Reports from the Reports menu. Quicken displays the Memorized Reports List.

2. Use the Up and Down Arrow keys to highlight the report that you want to access and press Enter. Note that from the Memorized Reports List you can edit a memorized report (press Ctrl-E to edit) and delete a memorized report (press Ctrl-D to delete).

Lesson 21

Budgeting with Quicken

In this lesson you will learn how to set up budget amounts for the categories that you use in Quicken.

Budgeting is a procedure for allocating income and expenses on a monthly basis and comparing those allocated amounts to actual amounts. For example, if you normally spend $50 per month for auto repairs, then you would allocate, or budget, $50 to a category for auto repairs and assign that category to all transactions relating to auto repairs. At the end of any given month, you can compare the actual amount spent on auto repairs to the budgeted, or allocated amount for auto repairs.

To use Quicken's budget capabilities, you must set up categories and assign transactions to categories. If you haven't been working with categories, you can set up categories now and either start assigning categories henceforth, or go back to prior transactions in the check register and assign categories.

Assigning Categories: To ensure that all transactions are assigned to categories, you can set one of the Quicken transaction settings to display an assign category message each time you record a transaction. To select this setting, type Y at the Require a category on transactions line from the Transaction Settings menu. (See Lesson 2 for more on the Transactions Settings menu.)

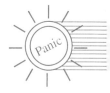

Entering Budget Amounts

Budget amounts are entered once—for monthly periods only. Quicken 5 enables you to enter monthly budget amounts and convert them to quarterly or yearly amounts (this feature is covered later in this lesson). Budget amounts can be changed at any time. To enter budget amounts:

1. From the Write Checks screen or any noninvestment register, select Set Up **B**udgets from the **A**ctivities pull-down menu. Quicken displays the Budgeting screen shown in Figure 21-1. The Budgeting screen displays categories on the far left side of the screen and monthly columns to enter budget amounts by category. (Note: Subcategories and accounts are also displayed if the Budget Subcats and Budget Transfers options are selected. These options are explained later in this lesson). Categories in the Budgeting screen are divided into two parts; *inflows* and *outflows*. Quicken compares total inflows to total outflows and displays the difference.

2. Move through the monthly columns. Type a budget amount (and press Enter) for some or all categories.

3. Press Ctrl-R to go back to the register or press Ctrl-W to go back to the Write Checks screen. (Budget amounts are automatically saved.)

Printing Budgets. Select Print Budgets from the File pull-down menu, or just press Ctrl-P, to print a copy of the budget amounts set up in the Budgeting Screen. Actual amounts will not be printed. (See Creating Budgeting Reports later in this lesson.)

Categories/Subcatagories   Monthly budgeting columns

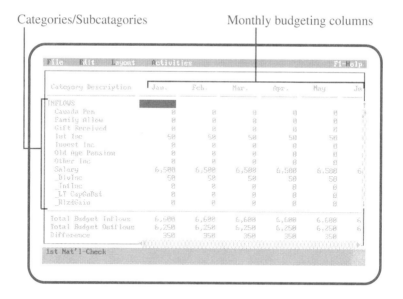

Figure 21-1. The Quicken budgeting screen for entering budget amounts.

Budgeting Subcategories and Transfers

When you access the Budgeting screen, subcategories and transfers (accounts) are not displayed. To set up budget amounts for subcategories and transfers, you must tell Quicken to display them on the Budgeting screen. To budget subcategories and transfers:

1. From the Write Checks screen or any noninvestment register, select Set Up **B**udgets from the **A**ctivities pull-down menu. Quicken displays the Budgeting screen shown in Figure 21-1.

2. From the **E**dit pull-down menu, select the Budget **S**ubcats or the Budget **T**ransfers option.

133

3. Quicken then displays all subcategories or accounts (if you chose to budget transfers).

4. Enter amounts for subcategories and transfers.

To quickly move through the Budgeting screen to enter budget amounts, use the keys explained in Table 21-1.

Table 21-1. Moving within the Budgeting Screen.

Keys	Function
Ctrl-Left/Right arrow	To move left or right one column
Tab	Move from month to month in the same row
Shift-Tab	Move back one month
Quote (") or Apostrophe Keys (')	Copies the amount from the previous month to the current month
Home	Moves to the beginning of an entry field or to the first column in a row of calculated fields
Home-Home	Moves to the first column in a row of entry fields or to the upper left corner of the screen from a calculated field
Home-Home-Home	Moves to the upper left corner of the screen from an entry field
End	Moves to the end of an entry field or to the last column in a row of calculated fields
End-End	Moves to the last column in a row of entry fields or to the lower right corner of the screen from a calculated field
End-End-End	Moves to the lower right corner of the screen from an entry field

Setting Up Budget Amounts from Actual Data

If you want to set up your budget amounts using actual amounts from your account registers, Quicken provides the AutoCreate option that automatically fills the columns in the Budgeting screen with the actual income, expense and transfer amounts for any time period in the current Quicken file. To set up budget amounts from actual data:

1. From the Budgeting screen, select the **A**utoCreate option from the **E**dit pull-down menu.

2. Quicken displays the Automatically Create Budget window shown in Figure 21-2.

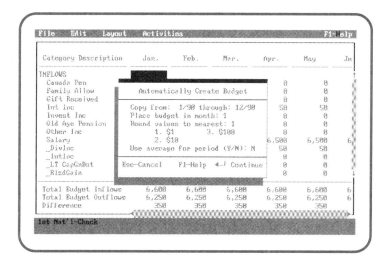

Figure 21-2. The Automatically Create Budget window.

3. In the Copy from field, type the time period that you want actual data extracted from. Then type the number of the first month in the Budgeting screen that you want actual data recorded in. For example, if you want actual data from a three month period recorded in June, July, and August in the Budgeting screen, you would enter **6**, since June is the 6th month of the year. (Note: The number of months of actual data must equal the number of months to be recorded in the Budgeting screen.)

4. Next, specify how actual amounts should be rounded.

5. Lastly, type Y if you want Quicken to compute income, expense, and transfer averages for any number of months and enter the average amounts in any month in the Budgeting screen.

6. Press F10 to set up budget amounts.

Copying Budget Amounts to Other Months

If your budget amounts are the same from month to month, you can use the Fill Right or Fill Columns options to copy budget amounts from one month to other months. To copy budget amounts to other months, follow these steps:

1. From the Write Checks screen or any noninvestment register, select Set Up Budgets from the Activities pull-down menu. Quicken displays the Budgeting screen shown in Figure 21-1.

2. From the Edit pull-down menu, select one of the following options:

Fill Right copies the highlighted budget amount to each month to the right in the *current* row.

Fill **C**olumns copies the highlighted budget amount column to all months to the right in *every* row.

3. Quicken automatically fills in each row/column.

Setting Up Budget Amounts that Occur Every Two Weeks

If you have budget amounts that occur every two weeks, instead of every month, you can use the Two Week option to set up those budget amounts. To set up budget amounts that occur every two weeks, follow these steps:

1. At the Budgeting screen, position the highlight bar in the category row that you want to budget on two-week intervals.

2. From the **E**dit pull-down menu, select the Two **W**eek option. Quicken displays the Set up 2 Week Budget window.

3. Type the amount you want to budget. Press Enter.

4. Type the starting date for the two-week interval.

5. Press F10 to set up two-week budget amounts in the Budgeting screen.

Changing the Screen Layout

The Budgeting screen is displayed in 12 monthly columns. You can change the layout of the screen to display budget amounts by quarter or by year. To change the layout of the Budgeting screen, select one of the following from the Layout pull-down menu:

> **Q**uarter displays budget amounts by quarter (four columns).

> **Y**ear displays the budget amounts by year (one column).

> (Note: You can enter budget amounts by quarter or by year. Then if you select the **M**onth option from the **L**ayout pull-down menu, Quicken distributes the budget amounts evenly across the monthly columns.)

Copying Budget Amounts from One File to Another

Quicken allows you to set up your budget amounts in one file and copy them to another file. To copy budget amounts from one file to another, follow these steps:

1. Select the Quicken file with the budget amounts that you want to copy to another file. (See Lesson 22 to learn how to select Quicken files.)

2. Select Set Up **B**udgets from the **A**ctivities pull-down menu in the Write Checks screen or any noninvestment register.

3. Select the Export Budget option from the File pull-down menu. Quicken displays the Save Budget to File window.

4. Type a name for the export file in the DOS File field and press Enter to create the file.

5. Select the Quicken file to copy budget amounts to.

6. Access the Budgeting screen.

7. Select the Import Budget option from the File pull-down menu.

8. Type the name of the file that you created in Step 4 and press Enter to copy the budget amounts in the Budgeting screen.

Creating Budget Reports

You can create Budget Reports that compare actual amounts with budgeted amounts and show the difference. Quicken provides two different Budget Reports: the Personal Monthly Budget Report and the Custom Budget Report. To create the Personal Monthly Budget Report, refer to Lesson 18. To create the Custom Budget Report, refer to Lesson 20.

In this lesson you learned how to use Quicken to set up budget amounts. In the next lesson, you will learn how to work with Quicken files.

Lesson 22

Working with Quicken Files

In this lesson you will learn how to set up new Quicken files, to back up, restore and copy files, and how to archive files and start a new year

Quicken works with one file at a time. A *file* is made up of accounts (as many as 255), all of which use the same categories, subcategories, classes, memorized transactions and reports, transaction groups, securities, security types, security goals, security prices, and electronic payees. Reports for Quicken files consolidate data from all or selected accounts within the file. When you start Quicken the first time and set up your first account, Quicken automatically creates a file for you. (Note to users of previous Quicken versions: In previous versions of Quicken, files were referred to as account groups.)

Setting Up a New Quicken File

You may need to set up a new Quicken file to keep track of transactions that are unrelated to your present file. To set up a new file, follow these steps:

1. Select Set Preferences from the Main menu and then select File Activities.

2. From the next window, select the Select/Set Up File option to display the Select/Set Up File window shown in Figure 22-1.

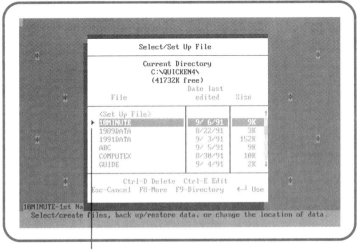

Selecting a file to use

Figure 22-1. The Select/Set Up File window.

3. Position the arrow on the <Set Up File> line and press Enter.

4. Quicken displays the Set Up File window shown in Figure 22-2.

5. Type a name for the new file (up to 8 characters; do not include symbols such as ." ∧ [ ] : < > + = ; ,). Press Enter.

6. Type the number that corresponds to the categories you want to use.

141

The drive and directory where new file is to be located

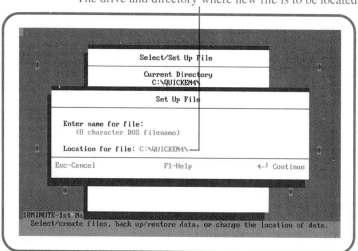

Figure 22-2. The Set Up File window for defining a new Quicken file.

7. Type the drive and directory where you want the data files created. (Remember, you must specify drive A or B to save the data to a floppy disk.) Press Enter.

8. Press Ctrl-Enter to add the new file to the Select/Set Up File list.

Editing and Deleting Quicken Files. You can edit or delete a file from the Select/Set Up File window. To edit a file, position the arrow on the file and press Ctrl-E to select the Edit option. To delete a file, press Ctrl-D to select the Delete option.

Selecting a File to Use

If you have more than one file, you must select the file that you want to use each time you start Quicken. To select a file to use, follow these steps:

1. Select Set **P**references from the Main menu and then select the **F**ile Activities option.

2. From the next window, choose the Select/Set Up File option to display the Select/Set Up File window.

3. Position the arrow on the file that you want to use and press Enter. (Press F9 if you need to change the directory to look for an account group.)

Changing the Drive and the Directory

You can change the directory where Quicken looks for your data files. To change the directory, follow these steps:

1. Select Set **P**references from the Main menu and then select the **F**ile Activities option.

2. From the next window, select the Set File **L**ocation option to display the Set File Location window.

3. Type the drive and directory where your Quicken data files are located and press Enter.

Backing Up Files

To protect yourself from losing important data, you should make a backup copy of each of your Quicken files on a regular basis. To back up *one* file, follow these steps:

1. Select Set **P**references from the Main menu and then select the **F**ile Activities option.

2. At the next window, select the **B**ack Up File option.

3. Quicken displays the Select Backup Drive window. Type the drive letter for the backup disk and press Enter.

4. From the file list, displayed next, use the Up and Down Arrow keys to position the arrow on the file that you want to back up.

5. Press Enter to begin the backup process.

To back up *all* files, follow these steps:

1. From the Write Checks screen or any register, select **B**ack up File from the **P**rint/Acct pull-down menu.

2. Type the drive letter for the backup disk.

3. Press Enter to begin the backup process.

Quick Backups. You can make a quick back up of the current file from the Main menu. Just press Ctrl-B to access the Back up option or Ctrl-E to access the Back up and Exit option.

Restoring a File

For hard disk users, you may need to restore a file if something happens to your hard disk. To restore a file, follow these steps:

1. Select Set **P**references from the Main menu and then select the **F**ile Activities option.

2. At the next window, select the **R**estore File option.

3. Quicken instructs you to insert your Backup Disk in Drive A. After your disk is inserted, press Enter.

4. From the file list, position the arrow on the file that you want to restore.

5. Press Enter to restore data to the file.

Copying Files

You may want to copy all or part of a Quicken file to start a new file. To copy a file:

1. Select the file that you want to copy from.

2. Select Set **P**references from the Main menu and then select the **F**ile Activities option.

3. At the next window, select the **C**opy File option to display the Copy File window.

4. Type the DOS file name for the new file and press Enter.

5. Type the path (drive and/or directory) where the new file will be located. Press Enter.

6. Type the beginning and ending dates for transactions to be copied and press Enter.

7. Type **Y** if you want to copy prior uncleared transactions, or **N** if you do not. Press Enter.

8. Type **Y** to copy all investment transactions, or **N** if you do not want investment transactions copied.

9. Press F9 if you want to set the maximum number of accounts that can be created in the new file. Quicken automatically sets the maximum amount to 64.

10. Press Ctrl-Enter to start copying.

11. When the copy procedure is complete, Quicken lets you continue using your original file or start using the new file.

Closing Quicken Files

At the end of the year or your accounting period, you may want to close your Quicken file before entering transactions for the new year. Quicken 5 provides you with two options for closing files: the Archive option and the Start New Year option.

Archiving Data

The Archive option copies all transactions from prior years to an archive file. For example, let's say that the current date is January 1, 1992; when you select the Archive option, all transactions dated December 31, 1991 and earlier are copied to an archive file. The current file remains untouched. To archive data from prior years, follow these steps:

1. Select Set Preferences from the Main menu and then select the File Activities option.

2. At the next window, select the Year End option to display the Year End window shown in Figure 22-3.

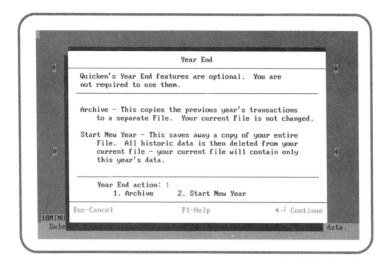

Figure 22-3. The Year End window to archive Quicken data.

3. Type 1 to select the Archive option.

4. Quicken displays the Archive File window. Quicken enters the file name, archive file location, and the archive transaction dates. Make any necessary changes to the Archive File window.

5. Press Ctrl-Enter to create the archive file.

Starting a New Year

The Start New Year option creates an archive file for all transactions from prior years and then deletes prior year transactions from the current file. (Note: Quicken never deletes uncleared transactions or investment transactions. After you perform the Start New Year procedure, your current file will contain only those transactions from the current year.)

To start a new year, follow these steps:

1. Select Set **P**references from the Main menu and then select the **F**ile Activities option.

2. At the next window, select the **Y**ear End option to display the **Y**ear End window.

3. Type **2** to select the Start New Year option.

4. Quicken displays the Start New Year window. Type a name for the archive file that Quicken will create and press Enter.

5. Make any necessary changes to the start date or the location for the current file.

6. Press Ctrl-Enter to create the archive file and delete transactions from previous years.

7. Specify which file you want to use; the current file or the archive file.

This lesson concludes your course through the *10 Minute Guide to Quicken 5*. Following this lesson, you will find the DOS Primer to help you with commonly used DOS commands and procedures.

DOS Primer

This section explains the basics of DOS and some of the procedures you'll use when working with it.

DOS is your computer's Disk Operating System. It functions as a go-between program that lets the various components of your computer system talk with one another. Whenever you type anything using your keyboard, whenever you move your mouse, whenever you print a file, DOS interprets the commands and coordinates the task. The following sections explain how to run DOS on your computer and how to use DOS to manage your disks, directories, and files.

Starting DOS

If you have a hard disk, DOS is probably already installed on the hard disk. When you turn on your computer, DOS automatically loads into your computer's electronic memory called *RAM* (Random Access Memory). If you don't have a hard disk, however, you must insert the startup disk that contains the DOS program files into the floppy disk drive before starting your computer.

Working with Disks

The basic DOS commands deal with three elements: disks, directories on the disk, and files in the directories. In this section you'll learn the basic DOS commands for working with disks.

Changing Disk Drives

Once DOS is loaded, you should see a *prompt* (also known as the DOS prompt) on screen that looks something like A:> or A> (or C:> or B:>) and tells you which disk drive is currently active. If you have a hard disk, the disk is usually labeled C. The floppy disk drives, the drives located on the front of your computer, are drives A and B. To activate a different drive:

1. Type the letter of the drive followed by a colon. For example, type a: .

2. Press Enter. The DOS prompt changes to show that the drive you selected is now active.

Formatting Floppy Disks

Before you can store files on a floppy disk, you must format the disk.

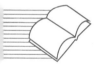 **What Is Formatting?** The formatting procedure creates a map on the disk that later tells DOS where to find the information you stored on it.

Format Caution. Be careful when formatting, because this procedure erases any existing information from the disk. Accidently formatting your hard disk will wipe out all program, system, and data files, so be careful.

1. Change to the drive and directory that contains your DOS files. For example, if your DOS files are in C:\DOS, type `cd\dos` at the C> prompt and press Enter. (For information on changing directories, skip ahead to the "Working with Directories" section.)

2. Insert the blank floppy disk you want to format into floppy drive A or B.

3. Type `format a:` or `format b:` and press Enter. A message appears telling you to insert the disk (which you have already done).

4. Press Enter. DOS begins formatting the disk. When formatting is complete, DOS may display a message asking if you want to name the disk.

5. To name the disk, type a name (up to 11 characters) and press Enter. A message appears asking if you want to format another disk.

6. Type `Y` if you want to format additional disks, then repeat all steps. Otherwise, type `N` to quit.

Using DISKCOPY to Make Backups of Program Disks

Before you install any program on your hard disk or run it from your floppy drive, make *backup copies* of the original program disks, to avoid damaging the original disks.

When you use the DISKCOPY command to copy the program disks, you don't have to format the blank disks before you begin. However, the blank disks must match the program disks in number, size, and density or DISKCOPY will not work.

 Protect the Disks. Before using DISKCOPY, make sure the original program disks are write-protected. For 3.5" disks, slide the write-protect tab so you can see through the window. For 5.25" disks, apply a write-protect sticker over the write-protect notch. Many program disks are write-protected by the manufacturer.

1. Change to the drive and directory that contains the DOS DISKCOPY file. For example, if the file is in the C:\DOS directory, type `cd\dos` at the `C:>` prompt, and press Enter.

2. Type `diskcopy a: a:` or `diskcopy b: b:`, depending on which drive you're using to make the copies.

3. Press Enter. A message appears, telling you to insert the source diskette into the floppy drive.

4. Insert the original program disk you want to copy into the specified drive and press Enter. DOS copies as much of the disk into RAM as RAM can hold. A message appears telling you to insert the target diskette into the floppy drive.

5. Insert one of the blank disks into the floppy drive, and press Enter. DOS copies the information from RAM onto the blank disk.

6. Follow the on-screen prompts to swap disks until DOS displays a message asking if you want to copy another disk.

7. Remove the disk from the drive, and label it to match the name of the original program disk.

8. If you need to copy another program disk, type Y and go back to Step 4. Continue until you copy all the original program disks.

9. When you're done copying disks, type N when asked if you want to copy another disk.

10. Put the original disks back in their box and store them in a safe place.

Labeling Disks. You should label disk copies with the names of the files and the current date. The pressure of a pen point can damage the fragile surface of a floppy disk. If you've already stuck the label to the disk, write on the label gently with a felt tip pen.

Working with Directories

Because hard disks hold much more information than floppy disks, hard disks are usually divided into directories. For example, if you're installing Quicken 5 for the first time, the Installation program suggests that you copy the Quicken 5 program files to a directory called QUICKEN5 on drive C. (If you already have an earlier version of Quicken on your system, it suggests the QUICKEN3 or QUICKEN4 directory.) This directory then branches off from the *root directory* of drive C, keeping all the Quicken 5 program files separate from all the other files on drive C. Directories can contain subdirectories as well.

153

The backslash (\) separates the names of the directories, giving DOS a *path* to follow in order to locate the directory at the end of the path. Use the backslash to separate all directories and subdirectories in a command line. A sample command line might look like this:

```
cd\forests\trees\maples
```

Making Directories

To create a directory using DOS, use the MD (Make Directory) command.

1. Change to the drive and directory under which you want the new directory to appear.

2. Type `md` directory, where *directory* is the name you want to use for the directory (up to eight characters).

3. Press Enter. The new directory now exists.

Changing to a Directory

Before you can work with the files in a given directory, you need to change to that directory.

1. Change to the drive that contains the directory.

2. Type `cd\`directory, where *directory* is the name of the directory you want to access. (For example, type `cd\nu`.)

3. Press Enter.

Displaying a Directory Name. If you change to a directory that you know exists and the directory name does not appear in the DOS prompt, type `prompt=$p$g` and press Enter.

Displaying a List of Files in a Directory

To see a list of files stored in the current directory, use the DIR (Directory) command.

1. Change to the drive and directory whose contents you want to view.

2. Type `dir` and press Enter. A list of files appears.

If the list is too long to fit on the screen, it scrolls off the top. You can view the entire list by typing `dir/p` (pause) or `dir/w` (wide). If you type `dir/p`, DOS displays one screenful of files; press Enter to see the next screen. If you type `dir/w`, DOS displays the list across the screen, fitting many more file names on screen.

Working with Files

Once you've activated (moved to) a directory, you can work with the files in that directory. You can:

- Copy a file from one drive or directory to another with the COPY command.

- Delete a file with the DEL command.

- Rename a file with the REN command.

To perform any of these operations, first change to the directory that contains the file(s) you want to work with. Type the appropriate command line, then press Enter.

- To copy a file, type `copy` *filename.ext* `d:` *directory**filename.ext* and press Enter. The first *filename.ext* is the file you want to copy, `d:`*directory**filename.ext* is the drive, directory (if any), and file name under which DOS will store the file copy.

Naming Copies. If you copy the file to the same drive and directory, the two *filename.ext* entries must differ. If you copy the file to a different drive or directory, you can omit the second *filename.ext* (the copy will have the same name as the original) or enter a new name.

- To delete a file, type `del` *filename.ext* and press Enter. When the confirmation message appears, type `Y` to delete the file or `N` to cancel the operation.

- To rename a file, type `ren` *filename.ext filename.ext* and press Enter. The first *filename.ext* is the current name of the file, and the second *filename.ext* is the new name you want to assign the file.

For more information about using DOS commands, see *The First Book of MS-DOS* or the *10 Minute Guide to MS-DOS 5*, both by SAMS.

Index

D

data disks, 2, 153
dates
   changing, 79
   ranges, 122
   locating by transactions, 32
decreasing accounts, 116
DEL command, 155
Delete option, 23, 45, 67, 76
Delcte Transaction option, 33, 82
deleting
   accounts, 23
   categories, 45
   checks, 81-82
   classes, 58
   files, 142, 155
   lines, 53
   transaction groups, 76
   transactions
      Check Register, 33
      memorized, 67
deposit transactions, 66
Describe Group window, 72-76
directories, 143, 153-157
DISKCOPY command, 152
disks, 2, 150-153
displaying budget amounts, 138
DOS, 149-150
drives, 143, 150

E

Edit Category screen, 44
Edit Class screen, 57
Edit option, 23, 82-83, 133-137
Edit pull-down menu, 30-33, 50-54
Edit/Setup Memorized Transaction
   window, 66
editing
   accounts, 23
   categories, 44
   classes, 57
   files, 142
   reports, 122
   split transactions, 53
   transaction groups, 75-76
   transactions
      Check Register, 32
      memorized, 66

Electronic Payment Settings
   option, 10-11
electronic register, 21
Enter Check Number window, 89
entering balances, 20
executing transaction groups, 77
Exit option, 144
exiting Quicken, 9
Expand feature, 122, 125
expanding report detail, 125
expenses
   computing, 136
   tracking, 48
Export Budget option, 139

F

features
   Collapse, 122-124
   Create Reports, 126
   Expand, 122, 125
   Memorized Reports, 130
   Move, 45
   Paste, 37
   QuickZoom, 122-123
File Activities option, 141-143
File menu, 132, 139
File/Print menu, 119, 122
files
   archive, 146
   backing up, 8-9, 143
   closing, 146
   copying, 138, 145, 155
   deleting, 142, 155
   editing, 142
   formatting, 150
   lists, 155
   new, 140
   renaming, 155
   restoring, 144
   selecting, 142
Fill Columns option, 136-137
Fill Right option, 136-137
filter transactions, 122
finance charges, 102
Find option, 30
First Time Setup window, 2
floppy disks, 2, 152
Function-Key menu, 3

159

Q–R

S